NINJUTSU

NINJUTSU

THE ART OF THE INVISIBLE WARRIOR

STEPHEN K. HAYES

Contemporary Books, Inc.
Chicago

Library of Congress Cataloging in Publication Data

Hayes, Stephen K.
    Ninjutsu : the art of the invisible warrior.

    Includes index.
    1. Ninjutsu.   I. Title.
UB271.J3H393   1984   355.5'48   83-26305
ISBN 0-8092-5478-6

Published by Contemporary Books, Inc.
180 North Michigan Avenue, Chicago, Illinois 60601
Manufactured in the United States of America
Library of Congress Catalog Card Number: 83-26305
International Standard Book Number: 0-8092-5478-6

Published simultaneously in Canada by Beaverbooks, Ltd.
195 Allstate Parkway, Valleywood Business Park
Markham, Ontario L3R 4T8 Canada

CONTENTS

This book is dedicated, with respect, to
Shinichi Urata,
whose persevering intention
created and built a secure family
upon the ashes left behind
by others.

Dr. Masaaki Hatsumi, grandmaster of the ninja and personal instructor of author Stephen K. Hayes.

ACKNOWLEDGMENTS

This book, and indeed the world's knowledge of the authentic ninja martial arts, would not have been possible without the generosity and openness of Dr. Masaaki Hatsumi, headmaster of the *Bujinkan dojo* network and grandmaster of the *ninjutsu* tradition.

In a time when the doors were closed and sealed for the majority of those who came in search of the warrior knowledge, Dr. Hatsumi and his senior instructors Fumio Manaka, Tsunehisa Tanemura, and Tetsuji Ishizuka permitted me entrance to their *dojo*. My own life was transformed as a result. For their graciousness those years ago I am forever grateful.

For all that he has given me, for all that he has helped me to see, for all that he has opened up to me, my heartfelt thanks go out to my teacher, *soke* Masaaki Hatsumi, *Byakuryu Oh.*

INTRODUCTION

Imagine that your family has worked for generations to develop a productive farm from a formidable forest, and your control now covers thousands of acres of fields and woods. Your immediate family lives with you in a comfortable dwelling, and your brothers and uncles and their farm workers live within a few hours of you, scattered throughout the family domain. You are considered just and reasonable by those who know you, and as long as water and weather hold out, your life and the future of your young ones will be secure.

One bright, warm morning you have loaded some carts with supplies from the village, and your attention is drawn to a noisy crowd of agitated farmers. Since you have their respect, they quickly and politely bring you up to date. It seems that this man's brother has just come in from the region beyond the mountains. That madman from the South has crossed their border with incredible numbers of troops and claims he won't stop until he has conquered this entire corner of our landmass. This traveler is to carry a signed promise from us to this brutal general. We must send a percentage of our produce to him and vow to do the same for three more years. He will send his henchmen to collect, or his army to destroy.

Our neighbors have sent messengers to the capital to ask our ruler for support, but that was just yesterday, and it will take weeks to make the journey. Who knows what might happen before the messengers reach the capital gates? Those mountain farmers over there can't offer much resistance. These attackers will be here in a little over a week.

What will you do to keep your lands and liberty and dignity in this savage and ungentle world?

This tale could take place in frontier America, medieval Europe, or colonial Africa. The ending might be fairly predictable: dirt farmers making a valiant but vain stand against the conqueror; all ensuing events recorded as "progress" or, at best, history in the making. Because this story takes place in feudal Japan, however, the ending can be surprisingly different.

You have heard tales of special men who live in the mountains and marshes to the South — mystics with incredible powers, aided by the *kami* spirits of their families. These legendary ones can destroy entire armies single-handedly, it is said. You know that you must find them.

For such a mission you trust no one. You set out with a servant for the isolated Iga province. Your grandfather had once told you of a temple he visited, where priests had interceded for him and had gone to these invisible ones with a

NINJUTSU: THE ART OF THE INVISIBLE WARRIOR

plea. For a hefty contribution, they had gotten your uncle out of treacherous hands. Now you seek this special temple, for salvation from treacherous hands.

There before you is the long, sloping gray-tiled roof supported by massive pillars of weathered cedar. You are in the bare temple grounds, looking at the structure. You proceed into the cool darkness, through the perfumed smoke, to kneel on a silk pillow and tap the edge of a bowl gong. Your misfortune echoes through the broken stillness on the vibrations of the reverberating brass before you to tell the gods you are here. Oh, blessed powerful ones, help me now to overcome oppressors.

The day is an eternity. You speak with one priest, who laughs quietly and mocks you. "Illusive ones the night produces? You must be speaking of the bats. Be patient and you will see our temple's bats." Another priest tells you that the supermen of the night are merely tales to delight children, usually told by old people. "You would better spend your time at prayer and meditation than seek those who do not exist." Other priests speak to you of philosophical thought. "This mad conqueror, perhaps the gods wish him success." "Perhaps it is the will of the universe." "Life is not ours to understand. It is only to be accepted."

You awaken conscious of your hunger. It is dark but for a few candles in the temple. You had fallen asleep kneeling on the woven mats of this sacred place. A priest is kneeling before you, watching you. He seems like a statue with living, peaceful eyes. "How may we help you, little brother?"

You speak again of your family's terror, of the urgency of these farmers who must face conquerors. From the priest's lips you hear the words that seem to tumble about you like slabs of plaster loosened by the thundering of war drums.

"You seek the ninja."

Ninja. The legendary mystic warriors of the mountain wilderness of feudal Japan were anonymous beings who had perfected the art of stealth, the art of invisibility, known as *nin-jutsu*. Their esoteric art enabled these living phantoms to walk on water, pass through walls, disappear at will, and read the innermost se-

crets of your heart, it is said. Their eyes would be watching you, but you would see no faces. Their ears would be listening to you when you thought yourself alone. And they were the masters of so very many ways of giving you your death, should that be the demand of the universal process.

You bow deeply and humbly to the old priest, whose subordinates had been testing you all day. As you bring your gaze up from the floor, you are startled to see a second kneeling figure beside the priest. This second man is bearded and dressed in the short coat and leggings traditional of wandering samurai warriors. Strangely, however, this man carries no sword.

This stranger watches you with hypnotizing eyes that seem to slide right inside your soul. When he speaks, his voice is low and his speech seems paced. It is a voice that could calm a raging bear, under different circumstances. Tonight the voice sends chills through you, as though it were coming from the grave.

"You may know me as Field Crow, for tonight. Your story interests me. We have had our people watching this neighbor of yours for some time now. And we have some of our agents in the ranks of this 'mad general.' You see, it is our way to know of such things before they are irrevocable or beyond our influence. We could resolve this dilemma for you, if you wish it so."

You somehow believe that this man can do what he says he can do. You bow and say that you now owe his family the life and honor of your family.

He speaks without returning a full bow. "We do not require so high a payment as that. Our families must eat, however. Will you deliver to this temple one-ninth of what this conqueror has demanded of you? In exchange we will save for you the other portion, as well as your family's lands."

You return home to your family and, with shaky confidence, proclaim that you will send no notes of promise to any mad generals. Then with great apprehension you wait.

And wait.

And wait.

Until nine days later, when you are approached by a laborer that you do not re-

member having seen before. He stands mop-
ping the perspiration from his neck and
forehead, making polite but boring conversa-
tion about some minor problems the workers
are having. Crows have been flocking to the
fields, giving them fits. You slowly turn to stare
at this strange little man and ask him what else
he knows of Field Crows and such.

He shrugs and says he doesn't know much
of anything, really. Just a lot of gossip, like a
story he was told. It seems that the clan way
over there was told that your family was mount-
ing a massive attack, with the intention of
taking over the entire corner of the landmass,
them included. Had them terrified of you. They
were supposed to pay you a percentage of their
produce for four years or you'd slaughter them
all.

The little man laughs with mock irony.

"Now isn't that funny, because some fellow
in the village was telling me that that clan was
supposed to be marching in on you if you
didn't pay.

"Some associates of mine, who have done
what you might call a little research, tell me
that this neighbor over the mountains, between
you and this other terrified clan, was making

two-way threats—east and west, and north and
south. Had all the families tricked into paying,
and the capital so confused with different
charges that they couldn't do anything. Seems
the sly one had already gotten some hostages
and was using his own men to pose as couriers
from all these 'enemies.'

"Rumor has it, however, that all has worked
out, with this evil one disappearing and the
hostages being released. You might not want to
mention the part about him disappearing,
though. Not quite yet, as he won't be disappearing until after he goes off to his bedchamber
tonight."

Stunned and shaken, you turn and call for
your brothers. They look up and are moving
toward you. You ask this strange messenger
behind you how all this was uncovered. Yes,
you had hired them, but it seems to have been
such a tangled web.

You hear no reply and turn to find the little
man gone. All you hear is the calling of some
crows out beyond the fields. Anyway, the question really was pointless. Who knows how they
knew everything? We are merely farmers and
tradesmen.

And they are the ninja.

1
ENDORSEMENT OF HISTORY

The warrior tradition known as *ninjutsu* has its roots in the martial, religious, political, and cultural histories of the ancient island nation of Japan. Conceived of during a time of political turmoil and total civil chaos, when day-to-day survival of one's family depended on personal strength, resourcefulness, and creativity, the ways of Japan's legendary ninja night warriors created an underground counterculture that provided the means and inspiration for prevailing despite overwhelming odds. The warrior tradition of the *shinobi* clans fostered the development of a living personal art that blended components of devastating combat skills, finely tuned powers of intuition and observation, and practiced abilities to transform intention into reality.

Roots of the Tradition

The essence of the tradition stemmed from the training methods of Japan's *shugenja* and *yamabushi* mountain warrior ascetics, who subjected themselves to the harrowing rigors of harsh wilderness living in order to realize and achieve the strength of the very mountains in which they dwelled. In the early part of the ninth century, the *shugendo* methods of cultivating power through the experience of trial

were expanded to include the *mikkyo* "secret doctrines" of enlightenment, then recently introduced to Japan from their far-off Himalayan sources.

Shugendo, the Japanese practice of encountering and overcoming personal fears and limitations in the wilderness of the mountains, was one of the fundamental roots of the tradition that would go on to be known as the art of *ninjutsu.* The current-era Japanese *yamabushi* pictured here observe the *mikkyo* fire ritual as a culmination of their practice sessions on Togakure Mountain.

The limitations of the English language and the Western cultural viewpoint lead us to describe that original *shugendo* concept as a curious mixture of religion and martial training. In reality, however, it was neither a religion nor a martial art in the sense that we use these terms today. *Shugendo* was the way of approaching enlightenment by repeatedly exposing oneself to the experience of overcoming dangers and potential death in the mountain wilderness. More than a religion, *shugendo* was a process of examining all religious systems and folk beliefs in order to find the universal elements that could lead to power and insight. More than a method of teaching troops or individuals the mechanics of battle tactics, *shugendo* was a process of going beyond technique to the higher experience of using the personal will as the ultimate tool for self-protection.

Art of Invisibility

As the history of the Land of the Rising Sun progressed through the ages, many of those who took to the practice of *shugendo* for personal reasons found themselves in a position of growing contention with the ever-changing governments and military powers that played a broad chess game with the villages, cities, and regions of feudal Japan. Vastly outnumbered by the conventional troops that attempted to subjugate them, prevented by law from defending their home communities and family domains, and blanketed by government tax restrictions that denied their freedom to construct and staff temples, shrines, and retreats, the wild holy men of the mountains more and more found the essence of their training being converted into a means of clandestine psychological and commando warfare.

Thus was born the legendary art of the ninja invisible warriors of south central Japan. A blending of the ways of guerilla warfare, espionage, and intelligence gathering; harmony with the cycles of nature; intense loyalty to one's family; and what the superstitious would call "sorcery," the art of *ninjutsu* developed as a warrior tradition unparalleled in the history of the world.

Black-clad ninja of legend blends with his surroundings and peers from behind a stone lantern pillar.

During the 13th-17th centuries in Japan, dozens of regional and familial *ryu* ("traditions" or "schools") operated out of the Iga and Koga territories southeast of the capital in Kyoto. Hidden away in their protective, inaccessible mountain abodes, the ninja families operated as powers in their own right and also aided conventional warlords who needed the assistance of the ninja's expertise in intelligence gathering and clandestine warfare.

Grim Reputation

It is an unfortunate reality that the art of *ninjutsu* and the ninja practitioners who developed the warrior tradition are often held in less than favorable light in the eyes and minds of the public the world over. This skewing of fact and philosophy is due perhaps primarily to the writings of long-ago Japanese historians who, as a part of the established samurai power structure, would naturally disdain anyone who opposed or threatened the status quo. If the samurai were to be seen as the guardians of the peace, then the ninja would have to be portrayed as terrorists and assassins. If unquestioning obedience and "knowing one's place" were what held feudal Japanese society together, then the ninja's free-flowing situational ethics and personal integrity would have to be presented as immoral treachery.

This gross misunderstanding and malignment has persisted even in modern times. Highly subjective historians as well as entertainment writers of Japan's postfeudal age have created a bleak and dismal portrait of the ninja in their attempts to glorify the samurai mentality. This prosamurai antininja attitude peaked during World War II in Japan when unquestioning obedience from the troops (the samurai way of thinking) was desired by the militarists who had taken control of the nation, and probing self-direction of the individual warrior (the ninja way of thinking) was feared. This attitude lived on after the war, carried in the hearts of the right-wing nationalistic old-guard leadership of the traditional martial arts in Japan. Many of the Western martial arts students and writers who found themselves in postwar Japan emulated and followed after this old guard unquestioningly, like puppies running after a sausage cart, and thereby transferred this abhorrence of martial individuality to the United States and Europe. Today, adventure novels, movies, and even daytime TV soap operas in the West are quick to add a ninja or two whenever a supposedly sinister and immoral character is needed for evil purposes.

The misunderstanding itself is a working part of *ninjutsu* training today in that it reminds the students of the impact and power of perspective in life. It could be said that one man's terrorist is another man's freedom fighter, if only through perspective and viewpoint. There are no absolutes. Even the founding fathers of the American republic could be labeled as terrorists and assassins if the commentator happened to be on the receiving end of George Washington's Christmas dawn surprise raid across the Delaware River.

The *Hakuhojo* White Phoenix Castle of Iga-Ueno, heartland of Japan's historical *ninjutsu* tradition. The Iga region was a bastion of families devoted to the ninja arts in the 15th and 16th centuries. During the 17th century the region came under the control of the Tokugawa Shogunate in Edo (ancient Tokyo), and Iga *ryu* ninja chieftan Hanzo Hattori became the new shogun's security advisor.

The Togakure Tradition

Today, the Togakure *ryu* of *ninjutsu* is the oldest remaining historically traceable ninja tradition in the world. The *ryu* was founded by the descendants of Daisuke Togakure, who studied with the *shugenja* of Togakure Mountain, north of Nagano, and later with the warrior wizard Kain Doshi of Iga. The *ryu*, currently in its 34th generation, was established in the late 1100s. Dr. Masaaki Hatsumi, of Noda City, Japan, is the grandmaster for the present generation, having inherited his title from his teacher, Toshitsugu Takamatsu, the 33rd grandmaster.

Along with the eight other warrior *ryu* for which Masaaki Hatsumi holds the title of *soke* ("head of the family" or, more commonly in

Togakure *ryu ninjutsu* 33rd grandmaster Toshitsugu Takamatsu trains his spiritual heir, Masaaki Hatsumi, in the clandestine ways of Japan's ninja combat method. It is interesting to note that in these photographs from the mid-1950s, the grandmaster and his students wear simple white judo training uniforms rather than the black suits traditionally worn today. In those postwar years the art of *ninjutsu* was kept totally underground as a secret tradition. Passersby would merely assume that the men were engaged in some sort of *jujutsu* sport training and would not suspect the true nature of what was being taught. It was only after the death of Grandmaster Takamatsu that public acknowledgment of the legendary art of *ninjutsu* was permitted.

the West, "grandmaster"), the Togakure *ryu* continues to thrive as an active training inspiration and guide in the modern world. The universal principles of mind and body work that characterized the original tradition are just as valid for society today as they were eight centu-

ries ago. In the *Bujinkan dojo* ("Divine warrior training hall") schools of Dr. Hatsumi, the following warrior skills are taught in a living and vibrant fashion:

  taiso (body conditioning)
  taijutsu (unarmed combat arts)
  bojutsu (stick fighting arts)
  tantojutsu (knife fighting arts)
  kenjutsu (sword fighting arts)
  shurikenjutsu (blade throwing arts)
  kusarifundojutsu (short-weighted chain arts)
  kyoketsu shoge (cord and dagger weapon arts)
  kusarigama (chain and sickle weapon arts)
  bisento (battlefield halberd arts)
  yarijutsu (spear fighting arts)
  hojutsu (firearm arts)
  ninki (specialized ninja tools)
  heiho (combat strategy)
  gotonpo (use of natural elements for evasion)
  meiso (meditation)
  shinpi (concepts of mysticism)

Training Today

Dr. Masaaki Hatsumi established his *Bujinkan dojo* group for the purpose of sharing the teachings of the original Japanese warrior tradition with seekers the world over. Combat efficiency and the pursuit of personal enlightenment are the two goals of the *dojo*'s training methods. Unlike the more popular conventional martial arts of Japan and East Asia, no sports competition, cultural patterning, or rote memorization is to be found in Dr. Hatsumi's training halls. In its full sense, the training begins with physical protection skills and then moves on through higher levels of awareness that allow the practitioner to manipulate dangerous situations before they develop to the point of no return.

In the Western world the Shadows of Iga society is the organization responsible for overseeing the training and licensing of *ninjutsu* instructors under the authority and guidance of grandmaster Masaaki Hatsumi. The Shadows

Author Stephen K. Hayes and his teacher, *ninjutsu* grandmaster Masaaki Hatsumi, working together to bring the values and powers of the authentic Japanese warrior traditions to the Western world. Through the grandmaster's *Bujinkan dojo* network, seekers around the world now have access to teachings that were once held secretly by a select few in the mountains of south central Japan.

of Iga *Bujinkan dojos* are recognized as the ultimate source for training in the authentic and historically proven methods of Japan's ninja night warriors. The combat skills of the following nine historical *ryu,* each headed by Dr. Hatsumi, are protected and disseminated by the Shadows of Iga *Bujinkan dojo* group:

Togakure ryu ninjutsu
Gyokko ryu koshijutsu
Kuki Shinden ryu happo hikenjutsu
Shinden Fudo ryu dakentaijutsu
Gyokushin ryu ninjutsu
Koto ryu koppojutsu
Gikan ryu koppo taijutsu
Takagi Yoshin ryu jutaijutsu
Kumogakure ryu ninjutsu

Those interested in the work of the Shadows of Iga society and in contemporary ninjutsu training in the Western world can write to the organization's international correspondence center at:

Shadows of Iga
PO Box 1947
Kettering, Ohio 45429

2

TRAINING AND CULTURAL VALUES

Today's modern Western society is no place for the cultivation of the skills and attitudes typical of Japan's feudal age samurai. Sadly enough, honor and proper respect for power rarely appear in the makeup of daily life. Waiters and sales clerks are routinely surly, as though convincing the customer of their equality or superiority were more important than providing service. Outrageous rudeness in roadway traffic is more than commonplace; it has become legendary in some parts of the Western world. U.S. laws are structured to discourage totally personal responsibility in self-protection by setting harsh fines and penalties for those citizens who too zealously defend their homes, families, and property from criminals who willfully go out of their way to attack and destroy someone else's established security.

The American notion that we are all "equal," regardless of individual intelligence, contribution to the community, capacity to love, and capability of destroying, has reduced our society to one in which many people no longer feel the need to be accountable for their choices or actions. Kick in the window and run off with the TV sets; the law does not permit anyone to kill or injure you for mere damage or theft of property. Raise your middle finger and spit out an obscenity; they cannot take physical

action against verbal assaults or you can sue them for battery. Firebomb the car of the worker who would not go out on strike with you; there is no way it can be proved in court, even though they know the perpetrator.

There are, of course, arguments for the course our progressing society has taken, through which granny-stabbers and baby-rapers are treated in institutions rather than subjected to the collective wrath of the family or clan to which the deceased granny or defiled baby once claimed kinship. Certainly, from one definition, it could be observed that we have left the days of barbaric "might makes right" thinking and entered a more benign age. Other definitions, however, would observe that the subtle and nefarious way that the unchecked growth of government has surreptitiously caused personal responsibility to become unfashionable, and in many cases illegal, thereby increasing the population's dependency on the government, is the height of calculated, destructive behavior.

The days of the samurai warrior elite are long gone, and with them went the need and responsibility for cultivating personal combat skills as a means of ensuring peace and cooperation in the community. Therefore, to train in potentially damaging physical techniques without counterbalancing with training in emotional and spiritual self-protection, is to place oneself in the excruciatingly awkward position of having awesome powers of retribution and no legal vent whatsoever for their application.

Ironically enough, the ninja's ancient combat method is perfectly suited to contemporary times in the Western world. The art was developed almost a millenium ago by persons who were forbidden by law to protect their families and communities, were continuously subjected to government pressures for higher and higher percentages of their work in the form of oppressive taxes, and were barred from teaching publicly their life ways and religions because of the prevailing superstitions and ignorance of the general public at large and the government's fear of seeing its ultimate authority questioned. Those less-than-complacent souls with eyes to see will perceive an identical period of temporary social corruption right now as we as a world let go of the old age and move into a new age. Therefore, the warrior tradition of *ninjutsu,* with its equal emphasis on physical, emotional, intellectual, and spiritual self-protection, is a method of great comfort for practitioners at all levels. Reliance on physical power alone is not only illegal today, but is also a dangerously weak philosophy that is totally lacking in the emotional and spiritual protection so necessary in these temporarily troubled times.

Training Structure

Ninja warrior training has as a primary goal the freeing of the practitioner from the strangling effects of artificial limitations, whether imposed by self or by external circumstances. This regaining of total freedom is described by the grandmaster of *ninjutsu* as a "return to zero," or attaining the formlessness of neutrality and omnidirectional potential. In the Oriental description of the structure of the universe, this quality is referred to as the "void," not in the sense of emptiness implied by the English word, but in the sense of *devoid* of shape or rigid predetermined manifestation.

This sense of formless spontaneity is some-

thing that dwells within all of us, so it is really nothing to be gained as such, but rather rediscovered after all the years of conditioning and attempting to fit in that we go through on our way to adulthood. A renewed sense of this ability to adapt and assume the appropriate shape for any situation is the essence of physical and intellectual ninja training today. Therefore, the more the student lets go of preconceived notions, rigid value judgments, uniform codes of behavior, etc., the more free and able he or she is to find a suitable means for handling any given conflict. This theory is quite the opposite of the conventional martial methods that require the student to drop all individuality and conform to a standard (*kata*) of movement and tactics.

Training exercises can be provided to encourage the experience of moment-to-moment matching of response to stimulus, but it should be remembered that the fundamentals, drills, simulated attack progressions, and striking target work are only pieces of the training progression and are not the art itself. Too many so-called martial arts have degenerated to the point where skillful imitation of a rigid standard is held to be the goal. The student is forced to give himself to the art. In *ninjutsu* training, the student is encouraged to take the art for himself and make it a part of his own personality.

Training begins with fundamental body movement for self-confidence and self-protection. Students practice methods of hitting the ground and rebounding safely, shifting and evading strikes and weapon hits, and learning to allow their bodies to be exactly where they need them to be. Next comes weapon familiarization, during which time the students learn to identify and apply natural body weapons and handheld tools for combat counters. The students then concentrate on recognizing their varying moods and emotional states when under the pressures of conflict or confrontation, allowing their natural breathing rhythms and body dynamics to be used as strengths rather than as weaknesses. Physical, emotional, and energy considerations of self-protection combat are then enhanced through the meditative channeling of the conscious awareness.

The *Dojo*

A proper *dojo* of the martial arts is far more than a mere "studio" or even "training hall," just as seeking the warrior's insights and enlightenment is different from "taking a few self-defense lessons." The Japanese word *dojo* can be understood more clearly by examining each of the two component characters that make up the single word. *Do* is literally translated as "the road" or "path"; in this case, it is the path or way of life that leads to ultimate all-piercing understanding. *Jo* is translated as "place." Therefore, a *dojo* is actually a place for the study and pursuit of the transcendental wisdom.

Indeed, it is possible to see all of life as a *dojo,* for it is the space in which the work toward mastery occurs, and not the room, building, or structure itself, that carries the title. In my own travels and training, I have visited many such spaces carrying the designation of *dojo,* and they have been as widely varied in qualities as the entire spectrum of all the martial training systems themselves.

The *dojo* of En no Gyoja and his fanatical *shugenja* followers, the forerunners of the ancestors of the warrior tradition of which my family and I are a part, is the vast eastern side of Togakure Mountain in the Joshinetsu Plateau of north central Japan. The focal point of the expansive *dojo* is in appearance little more than a roughly cleared creek- and cedar-lined patch of windswept grasses, and yet just moving through the area provided me with insights that had eluded me totally for my first 15 years in the martial arts. So charged with power was that *dojo* acreage that my consciousness was literally forced to see and acknowledge the higher significance of the way the tradition of the *ryu* I belong to permitted my teachers and me to do things that other observers quickly dismissed and labeled "unexplainable." Two tiny, ancient, weathered wooden signposts, their faded Japanese characters barely visible now, are all that identify the *dojo* for the few tourists who venture up there.

During the years of my apprenticeship in Japan the personal *dojo* of my teacher was a roughly paneled room that adjoined a Western-style conversational parlor in the back of his home. Though very small by conventional standards, the *dojo* of the grandmaster was more than adequate in size for the handful of students that the man had agreed to teach in those days. Racks of pegs along the walls held scores of weapons, some of them padded as training aids, others the actual killing tools

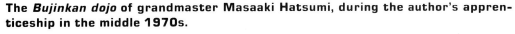

The *Bujinkan dojo* of grandmaster Masaaki Hatsumi, during the author's apprenticeship in the middle 1970s.

The *kamiza,* or "spiritual seat," of the author's personal training hall. From left to right, the central focal point of the *dojo* incorporates a portrait of Masaaki Hatsumi, the author's teacher; calligraphy by Dr. Hatsumi that stresses awareness and safety in the training hall; artwork by the grandmaster that symbolizes the roots of the warrior tradition in Japanese history; greenery signifying a closeness with all of nature; a power talisman from the Togakure Mountain shrine; a wooden housing for the mirror that symbolizes the transiency and illusory nature of all things; a power talisman from a shrine in the author's Japanese home city of Kumamoto; artwork by Grandmaster Hatsumi that depicts the Indian sage Daruma Taishi, who introduced the concept of meditation to China; calligraphy that stresses adaptability, freedom from limitations, and ever-growing realization in combat and life; and a portrait of Toshitsugu Takamatsu, the teacher of grandmaster Masaaki Hatsumi. Beneath the *kamidana* shelf is a *shimenawa* rope from the author's wife's family to indicate that the area has been blessed and empowered.

themselves. Shrines symbolic of the ancestry of the *dojo* and the warrior guardians of the Japanese tradition were perched high up on the walls near the ceiling. A large portrait of our teacher's teacher looked down on the training area from a position of respect high up on the *kamiza* central focus wall. The *dojo* was charged with the spirit of the grandmaster himself, as well as the energy of his dedicated *uchi deshi* ("home students") who trained there. Although the small room was in fact the only place in the world where the authentic warrior art of *ninjutsu* was being taught at that time, passersby in the street had no way of telling the grandmaster's building from the ordinary neighboring structures around it. No signs proclaimed it as a ninja training hall, nor was the external structure at all indicative of the

knowledge of the ages being disseminated inside.

Since the spring of 1980 the teachings of Dr. Masaaki Hatsumi's *Bujinkan dojo* have been increasingly available to the Japanese, European, and American public. Though the full range of ninja skills, knowledge, and power is still reserved for a select few individuals in the world, the pragmatic methods of *ninjutsu* unarmed combat, stick fighting, blade work, and flexible weapons are at last available to an expanding number of practitioners who have been invited to study in the *Bujinkan dojo* branch training halls around the globe.

Many of the clubs and training groups practice in facilities donated by military and police units that incorporate the individual combat methods into their members' training regimen.

Special tactics squads and antiterrorist teams in the United States, Western Europe, the Middle East, and Japan have adopted the thorough and history-tested technique system as a welcome expansion of their community-protecting capabilities.

Selecting a Dojo

For the reader who is not yet formally training in the martial arts and is considering enrolling in a training hall, here are a few suggestions to aid in deciding on a *dojo.*

Thoroughly check out all the schools in your area. Shop around for exactly what you are looking for, just as you would when considering the purchase of an automobile or a house or personal investment in a career. Look at what is offered, holding in mind what it is you want. There are schools that specialize in sports competition. There are groups specializing in physical recreation. There are *dojos* specializing in historical preservation of ancient cultures. There are indeed many approaches to the martial arts, and they are widely varied.

Beware of schools claiming to provide a little of everything. The wise consumer would probably shy away from buying a car promoted as having all the combined features of a sports racer, a pickup truck, a formal limousine, an armored personnel carrier, and an economy gas-saver. It is equally impossible to combine training in sports competition, cultural tradition, and pragmatic self-protection. Keep looking until you find the school that is right for you.

Visit the schools you are considering joining. See if the feel of the training hall is comfortable, confidence inspiring, and positive. You will be spending a lot of time in whichever school you choose, so you want to be sure that you will be safe, well treated, and happy there. Be honest with yourself. The *dojo* you choose will become a part of all that makes up your personal identity and image. You will want to be affiliated with a training group to which you can point with pride when identifying yourself.

Find out about the teacher in any school you are thinking of joining. He or she should give you a feeling of confidence based on his or her martial skills and personal bearing. The teacher should embody and live up to what is said to be taught in the school. Talk with some of the active students in the *dojo* to get their insights on the teacher you are considering. Check with personal associates in your community to get a fuller idea of the teacher's reputation. Find out where the teacher got his or her knowledge and then weigh all the information items together with your own gut-level feelings about this person.

Be wary of the unfortunate fact that black cloth belts can be purchased through the mail by anyone, regardless of training background. Fraudulent misrepresentation of authority through falsification of teaching rank is one of the greatest problems facing the martial arts community today. There are persons in the world posing as everything from karate champions to *kung-fu* grandmasters without the benefit of anything even remotely substantial to back their claims. The case is even more alarming with imitators pretending to be *ninjutsu* instructors, as there are so very few persons in the world licensed by the grandmaster to teach the art. You owe it to youself to be careful.

The *Sensei*

Any established *dojo* and group of students is but the reflection of a *sensei,* that person who shares his or her knowledge in the role of teacher. The Japanese word *sensei* can be understood more clearly by examining each of the two components that make up the single word. *Sen* is translated as "ahead" or "before," and *sei* is translated as "to live." The term *sensei* means "one who has lived through the experience before us." In this case the teacher is identified not as one who merely hands out information, but as one who serves as a life model.

The term *sensei* is therefore a one-way label, in that it is used only by a student to address or refer to his or her teacher with respect. A proper teacher never uses the term *sensei* to refer to himself or herself. To flaunt the title "life role model" is to behave with an audacity that shouts of either naivete or pompousness. A person who realizes the weight of the responsibility of running an authentic *dojo* will use verb forms of teaching words or some title that reflects a hierarchical position in his or her own teacher's martial tradition for identification. The word *sensei* will never appear on the calling card or stationery of one who has been trained in the higher orders of the warrior arts.

Likewise, the title of "master" is even more rigidly one-way. The Japanese word for master of the martial arts is *meijin. Mei,* the first of the two written characters that make up the word, means "name," and *jin* means "person." Figuratively translated as "person who has made a name for himself," the title of master could be used by students or practitioners only to refer to the great achievement and life work of another person. It would be scandalously self-glorifying to use the title of master on one's own calling card or stationery, and the willful personal adoption of the term as a title or rank would open even a legitimate master to harsh ridicule.

The seemingly inordinate amount of respect and ceremonial politeness that is often paid the teachers of Oriental martial arts is often grossly misunderstood in the Western world. Ritual for the sake of ritual is pointless abstraction, in the East just as it is in the West. There are good reasons for showing a lot of deference to a true master teacher, just as there are no real reasons for venerating a person who claims master status while being only a few steps ahead of the students he is collecting.

Extreme politeness could stem from very real feelings of fear and awe. If one has observed the master teacher to have the capability of deadly skills, then politeness may be well in order to avoid offending the teacher and causing him the need to reestablish the weight and validity of his reputation at the erring student's expense. Fear could also be born of the realization that the teacher could at any time choose to cast a student out, thereby forever eliminating that student's chances of gaining the knowledge taught in the *dojo.*

Extreme politeness could be generated through intense feelings of respect, thankfulness, and love for the teacher. If one has experienced great life changes while under the guidance of a teacher, then politeness and the insistence that others also demonstrate suitably respectful behavior around that teacher will probably be a quite natural aspect of the student-teacher relationship. In the martial schools that go beyond the limits of coaching paying strangers in mechanical concepts, the *dojo* often becomes a strong family group, with the teacher seen as the venerable head of the close-knit gathering of followers.

Another highly realistic impetus toward the great deference paid a master teacher is the fact that the performance of errands, little courtesies, and voluntary work may be the best means of getting the most knowledge possible out of the teacher. What might appear to be slavishly selfless actions on the part of a student could indeed be a reflection of the student's astute awareness that the less time the teacher spends on daily chores and routines, the more time the teacher has to share knowledge. Every moment the master teacher spends in earning a living, weeding the garden, fixing meals, washing clothes, or fulfilling all the other mundane necessities of life is time not spent teaching or doing research that will provide more to teach. The students of a master teacher with much knowledge to share will gladly see to it that the teacher's daily chores are taken care of so that the teacher can devote full attention and time to the job of giving the students what they need and desire.

Training Hall Etiquette

Historically, a knowledge of, and ready willingness to demonstrate, proper respectful modes of etiquette were crucial to survival in a warrior-dominated society. If every person encountered were skilled to some degree in and well equipped for deadly combat, one would find it much more prudent and convenient to observe those minimal courtesies that would ease potential frictions in daily life dealings with others. Therefore, proper modes of etiquette were among the first items of knowledge taught to new students as they entered the *dojo* ranks in centuries past. Etiquette was not mere formality; it was necessary for survival.

Certainly, developing effective skills of efficient self-protection in contemporary international society has nothing whatsoever to do with practicing 17th-century Japanese etiquette formalities, any more than learning modern army drill field commands will make one a better marksman. Feudal Japanese society was highly structured in terms of rank in society and government, and therefore a highly stylized system of ritual politeness evolved and was mandatory for all but social outcasts. This strict and rigid system was, however, eventually abandoned with the military dictatorship of Japan and the end of the samurai class at the time of the Meiji Restoration of imperial power. In the Japan of today militaristic formality is a relic one now finds only on television period dramas depicting the long-dead samurai age of centuries past.

It is therefore totally unnecessary to require

The Japanese *ritsurei* standing bow of greeting, thanks, or departure. The back is kept straight, and the body bends from the hips approximately 45 degrees. The hands are held at the sides of the thighs or can slide down the front of the thighs for females performing the bow. Contrary to what is sometimes taught in martial arts schools across the globe, it is not necessary to keep your eyes riveted on the person opposite you. Your natural awareness and peripheral vision will allow you to pick up any unsuspected hostile actions, should they occur in the middle of the bowing process.

American, European, and even contemporary Japanese students of the martial arts to behave as though they were the minions of some ancient Japanese *daimyo* warlord who had the power to order them to die without question. Normal street etiquette in Japan does provide for bowing and Japanese language salutations, but merely as parts of life in Japan. There is nothing about martial arts training itself, however, that requires one to behave like a Japanese if one is not in Japan. For an American teacher of the combat martial arts to insist that his American students bow to him, look at the ground when holding open doors for him, and speak in clipped Japanese terms even when encountering him in shopping malls or fast food drive-ins is the height of silliness and unnecessary game playing. Such behavior usually has the effect of distracting both the student and teacher from the real essence of personal warrior power as a way of life.

For teachers and students who enjoy the practice of the Japanese martial arts as a cultural exercise alone, antiquated behavior patterns can be adopted and enacted as part of the fun, even though such actions have nothing to do with self-defense. Japanese etiquette elements could also be observed at certain times in the *dojo* so as to familiarize the students with appropriate modes of behavior that will be necessary when visiting the teacher of one's own teacher in his *hombu* central training hall in Japan. In the case of Dr. Masaaki Hatsumi's *Bujinkan dojo,* the grandmaster requires all students who are candidates for the higher rank licenses to visit Japan. There the student can get to know the master teachers of the tradition, and those teachers can get to know the foreign student. A working knowledge of Japanese *dojo* etiquette is therefore essential for becoming a part of the worldwide *Bujinkan dojo* family. Again, as in the past, proper etiquette is a matter of survival for those who would be warriors.

Dojo *Guidelines*

The following guidelines are suggestions for making your visit to a Japanese *dojo* a more

A

The Japanese *zarei* kneeling bow is used when a more formal salutation is appropriate.

B

C

The left and then the right knees are lowered to the floor with the toes of both feet gripping the floor surface. The feet are then extended and flattened as the seat is lowered onto the heels.

E

Be careful to avoid folding or overlapping the feet or toes. From this *seiza* kneeling posture, lean forward and place the left palm in front of the left knee and then place the right palm in front of the right knee.

D

F

(Continued on next page.)

G

With your back and neck straight, lower your face toward the triangle formed by your outstretched hands and immediately return to the upright position.

I

Bring your right hand back to your right thigh and then your left hand back to your left thigh.

H

J

K

To rise, lift your seat and grip the floor with the toes of both feet. Bring your right foot into position on the floor and then straighten your left knee to rise.

M

The entire bowing procedure should be a series of smooth and flowing actions, each one leading into the next. Avoid abrupt or jerking motions.

L

N

rewarding experience as a result of increased confidence through knowledge of the basics of training hall decorum. If you are already aware of what is expected of you, you will not have to waste time trying to figure out what is or is not appropriate behavior and will have that much more energy to direct toward learning as much as possible.

First, remember that bowing in Japan is a salute of greeting, thanks, or departure, and not a symbol of subservience or religious reverence as it is in the West. Observe others in the training hall to get a better idea of when to bow, and if there is ever any question as to whether a bow is needed, bow anyway just to be safe. It is far better to be thought of as overly polite than as disrespectful, uncaring, or boorish. Bowing to things, while perhaps comical to the Western mind, is a part of the procedure as well. A bow to the *kamiza* central focal point of the *dojo* or to appropriate pictures of master teachers and past sages when entering or leaving the *dojo* is never out of place.

Keep words to a minimum in the *dojo*. While in America a terse single-word reply to a superior or teacher might be considered abrupt or offensive, in Japan brevity is definitely the best way to go. Excessive wordiness can be annoying to the Japanese, so do not be concerned with memorizing long strings of formal responses. It is the teacher's job to talk, and it is up to the student to pick up as much knowledge as possible.

Stay alert at all times. A *dojo* can be a dangerous place for the unwary, with fists, sticks, swords, and the like being moved through the training hall, which Westerners always feel is too small and crowded a space. If momentarily not engaged in training, rest away from the action in a neutral standing position with your arms at your sides. Never lean against a wall or shift all your weight to one crossed leg, where you can be trapped in immobility if you suddenly have to move to avoid a fellow student. When sitting, take a *seiza* kneeling pose or at least a crossed-leg lotus position to avoid extending your legs, where they could be a dangerous obstacle to others and a risk to your own health.

Enjoy the training activities from moment to moment as they unfold. In general, allow yourself to concentrate totally on all that you are learning, while employing awareness and good common sense, and you will have no problem with etiquette matters. Any good teacher will be able to recognize the enthusiasm and commitment that comes with 100 percent involvement in the training experience, and that excitement and inspiration is what any master is working to bring out in the student. Proper etiquette comes naturally because you have become an integral part of all that your *dojo* is.

3
TAISO BODY CONDITIONING

Health, vitality, and vibrant life are all integral parts of the warrior tradition, and an awareness of one's health is consistent with the overall training concept embodied in the *ninjutsu* combat method. Indeed, the first step toward mastery of self-protection skills is a working understanding of how to protect oneself from oneself. In contemporary society there are so many tempting and alluring habits, foodstuffs, chemicals, conveniences, and diversions that it is not at all difficult to find oneself led astray from a life of health, strength, and proper protection of the self. Soon both mental and physical health can be in a state of ruin without our awareness of the gradual process. If an individual is constantly sucking in clouds of nicotine-laden smoke, pulling in nosefuls of chemical dust for recreation, indulging in unbalanced eating and drinking habits, and looking for all the shortcuts to avoid physical action or taking on physical training routines that are detrimental to the body, it is absurd for him to study self-defense against external attackers. This person's most dangerous enemy is himself.

The ninja's physical conditioning program consists of first becoming aware of self-created limitations and then conscientiously working through them. The natural tendency of the body is to descend into the debilitating inertia of inactivity. Without the stimulation of active use, the muscles atrophy and lose their strength, the joints fuse and lose their flexibility, the lungs constrict and reduce their vital capacity, the heart grows weak and the circulatory system loses its dynamic nature, and the body becomes addicted to consuming and storing more and more needless fuel, which it converts to fatty tissue.

As a means of combating this tendency toward disintegration, the art of *ninjutsu* includes training methods that provide a means for developing muscular strength, maintaining body flexibility and suppleness, stimulating the respiratory and circulatory systems, and moderating the food intake. Regular training in the fundamentals of the ninja's *taijutsu* unarmed fighting does, of course, provide a good basis for maintaining strength, flexibility, aerobic capacity, and appropriate body weight. For many students, however, the specialized disciplines of *ninjutsu* body conditioning are necessary tools for overcoming and balancing out unhealthy states developed through years of detrimental habits that stemmed from a lack of understanding.

Dietary Considerations

The first steps toward a healthful diet are to reawaken to an attunement with what the body tells us it needs and then to become aware that social customs and convention are not always the best indicators of what constitutes good eating habits. These two steps are not necessarily as easy as we would like them to be. Ingrained habits take years to work their way into the personality and perceptions. Once a part of our personal makeup, they are not instantly released or effortlessly replaced with a few minutes, or even a few months, of work. Perseverence and commitment are required.

Diet must be brought into consistency with the overall concept of the warrior way of life. Students are urged to respect the universal laws and live in harmonious accord with nature. As a guideline for Western students, the current grandmaster of *ninjutsu* offers for consideration his own diet preferences in Japan. The bulk of his diet is made up of uncooked vegetables, *genmai* (unpolished rice), *tofu* (soybean curd), *goma* (sesame seed), *natto* (fermented soybeans), *miso* (bean paste) soups, and small fish, consumed bones and all. Grandmaster Hatsumi also strongly recommends totally avoiding foods that have been prepared with large quantities of sugar or salt.

Westerners who have access to sources of Japanese food supplies could follow the advice of grandmaster Masaaki Hatsumi to the letter by literally adopting the macrobiotic diet plan referred to above. A more likely and perhaps more reasonable or pragmatic plan for Americans and Europeans is to observe the cardinal principles of those diet suggestions while structuring meals around locally available food types. Grains from one's own area can be substituted for the rice, beans from the surrounding area could be found to supply more of the necessary nutritional qualities than soybeans shipped from another region, and fruits and vegetables indigenous to the area will often supply needed trace elements that balance or blend with other foods native to the locale.

It is also highly important to note that Dr. Hatsumi advocates a diet of *preference,* not one based on religious conviction or a feeling of moral superiority. Anyone aggressively demanding a complexly structured specific diet plan, even under conditions that make the diet impossible, is only creating a new artificial limitation that will someday get in the way and cause a self-generated difficulty or hardship. As with all other aspects of the *ninjutsu* combat method, moderation is a consideration as well.

Body Flexibility

The ninja's *junan taiso* body flexibility training provides for the structural freedom, suppleness, responsiveness, and speed required for the effective application of the techniques typical of the *ninjutsu* combat method. The muscles and joints are worked to enhance their natural elastic qualities through relaxed stretching exercises. This type of conditioning is characterized by maintaining poses that stretch the muscles and flex the joints for several seconds, eventually allowing them to extend to the full natural limits for a healthy body.

The following *junan taiso kyuho* nine fundamental stretching and limbering exercises are recommended as a good basic group of joint and muscle flexibility builders. As a minimum, the *kyuho* can be performed in just over 10 minutes as a preliminary warm-up before *taijutsu* training. The *taiso* can also be considered a full workout in itself, with more time spent on each exercise, and additional variations and supplementary stretches added.

When working through the *junan taiso kyuho,* remember to keep your breath moving in and out of your lungs in a natural and appropriate rhythm for each exercise performed. Ease your body into each stretch, avoiding any harsh or jerking motions.

Exercise 1

Engage the muscles of the neck by rotating the head in full horizontal circles from the top of the neck where it meets the head, as well as from the base of the neck where it meets the shoulders.

Next, turn the head from side to side as far as it will go and lift and lower the chin vertically as far as it will go. Keep the teeth clenched when performing all variations of this first exercise.

A

B

C

Exercise 2

Work the stretching and twisting action on down the spine, holding in your mind the image of freeing each individual vertebra, from the base of the skull to the top of the tailbone.

Hold your hips in position, facing directly forward, and work at pivoting your shoulders from side to side as far as they will go. Do not allow the hips to join in the turning movement of the shoulder assembly, or the effects of the exercise will be greatly reduced. Work several repetitions on each side, taking the shoulders a little farther each time.

Next, work through the same exercise again, this time leaning as far back and then as far forward as possible each time you turn your shoulders to the side. Slowly and gently go through several repetitions on each side.

C

A

D

B

E

(Continued on next page.)

F

G

Exercise 3

Engage the muscles of the shoulders and upper back by lifting and rotating both arms, one after the other, with a movement reminiscent of elbowing one's way through thick jungle foliage, and then roll the arms forward and backward as though swimming.

Next, reach back over one shoulder while reaching up from beneath the other shoulder, and clasp the hands together. Move and shift the arms and shoulders as much as possible before releasing the hands and reversing the arms to clasp the hands from the opposite sides.

A

B

C

(Continued on next page.)

D

E

F

G

H

I

(Continued on next page.)

(Continued on next page.)

P

Q

R

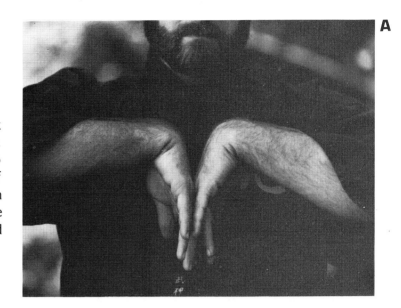

Exercise 4

Work the wrists and finger joints back against themselves for increased flexibility. Bend the wrists down, back, and from side to side as far as possible to create the effect of someone else trying to injure your wrists. With the same gentle but persistent action, lever the fingers up over the backs of the hands and fold them down over the palms.

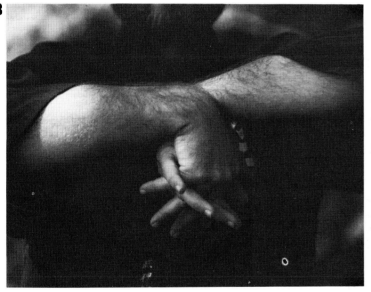

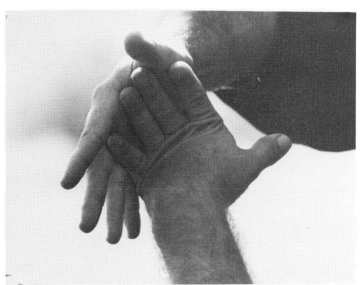

Exercise 5

Spread the feet as far apart as possible while still maintaining flat-footed balance. Press down on both thighs with the palms of the hands and twist from side to side to stretch the muscles of the back and move the bones of the spine.

From there, rock gently from side to side, moving as far to the sides and as low as possible while keeping the feet firmly on the ground.

Next, roll the toes of the extended foot up to allow the thigh and calf to stretch into an extended position along the ground. For maximum flexing effect, keep the torso upright, in typical *taijutsu* fighting form, rather than allowing the shoulders to lean forward in comfort.

A

B

C

D

(Continued on next page.)

Exercise 6

Allow the feet to slide out to both sides, spreading your legs as far as possible while lowering your torso. Use the natural pull of gravity to assist you in going a little farther each time you do the exercise. From this extended split position, lower your seat onto the ground and work your torso forward and down over both knees and to the center. Keep your back as straight as possible to derive the maximum benefit. Do not hunch your back over in order to lower your face to your leg.

Exercise 7

Sitting on the ground, pull your feet in toward the centerline of your body, place them sole to sole, and work your heels in as close to your torso as possible. Push both knees down as far as they will go toward the ground.

Keeping your back as straight as possible, lean forward over your folded legs and lower your body trunk toward the ground several times, going a little farther each time.

From that position, work on ankle flexibility by shifting forward to bring your torso up into position over your joined feet. Keep your back as straight as possible while flexing your knees to rise up and lower yourself back down several times in succession.

A

B

C

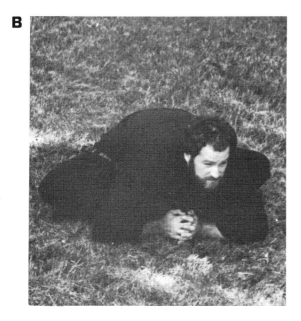
D

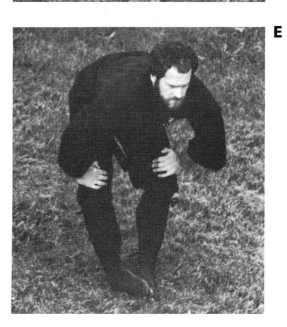
E

Exercise 8

Sitting on the ground push your feet forward so that they extend out in front of you side by side. Lean forward over your legs, keeping your back as straight as possible, and reach out over your toes to pull yourself down as far as you can. Repeat the exercise several times, taking each repetition a little farther.

From this forward folded position, lean back and extend your straightened arms as far back as possible, keeping them in alignment behind your shoulders as you lower them. Repeat the procedure several times, allowing yourself to relax a little further into the exercise each time. To finish this eighth exercise, lower your back to the ground and roll onto your shoulders, allowing your knees to rise up and then lower into position along the sides of your ears.

A

B

C

D

E

Exercise 9

Pull your legs beneath you in the Japanese-style *seiza* kneeling position with your hands resting in your lap. Close your eyes or keep them in an unfocused state and slowly take a deep full breath. Totally fill your lungs and then hold that breath for as long as is comfortably possible. After holding the breath, gently release it, letting it fall out from the center of your body. When you feel that all the air has been released, tighten your abdominal muscles up and in to force the last of the air out. From that point, relax the abdomen and flex your ribs without taking in any air, so as to cause your stomach to pull in and create a hollow cavity in its place. Hold this deflated state for as long as is comfortably possible before relaxing and allowing the air to rush into the lungs naturally. Repeat the exercise two more times, spacing each of the three deep breaths with a natural breath cycle.

After completing the three processes, continue to breathe normally and spend a few moments in concentrated awareness of building up and channeling the body's physical strength energy.

Muscle Conditioning

In balancing counterposition to the nine fundamental flexibility exercises are conditioning routines designed to build muscle strength for power. With these exercises the muscles are overloaded and worked to the point of fatigue or final unresponsiveness as a means of calling for more power to be developed. In response, the body becomes used to the strength output needed and eventually accommodates by building up to the point where the new demands can be handled routinely.

Perhaps one of the most effective muscle conditioning exercise concepts is to design the training to reflect skills and powers that will actually be needed later on. For training, you exaggerate whatever it is you will need to do and then repeat the exercise to your own limit. For example, if you occasionally need to climb a 30-foot vertical rope, practice for power by climbing up and down a 50-foot rope several times per workout session.

The following fundamental exercises are advised as a good set of overall muscle stimulators and power builders. Unlike the stretching exercises, the power builders should not be performed to maximum output and fatigue every day of the week. Students are advised to work the exercises on an every-other-day basis, to allow their bodies to rest and build up. It is also suggested that these exercises not be used as pretraining warm-ups, as the fatigue sensation will hinder the effective practice and development of proper fighting skills. Save the strenuous muscle work for after the reaction drills, accuracy training, and creative response practice, and use the conditioning work as a final burnout. As with the stretching and flexibility work, proper breathing rhythms are necessary to support the work of power buildup.

Leg Conditioning

For increased leg power to deliver stronger kicks, to perform longer leaps, and to facilitate more effective angling and powerful footwork, the calves, knees, and thighs can be exercised in ways that isolate the muscle groups that require strengthening.

The entire leg can be exercised by pushing against a stationary target and accommodating the slow forward movement with back

Leg flexing against a stationary target for strength development.

pressure resistance from tensed arms against the target. From a crouched and coiled position with the palms of the hands pressed against a tree trunk, solid wall, or pillar, slowly engage the muscles of your entire leg in an uncoiling action against the target. Work the exercise until your legs and their joints are fully extended. Relax and repeat the exercise several times.

The muscles of the thighs can be developed by extending the legs into weighted targets from a reclining position on the ground. On

(Continued on next page.)

Using the two training partners to assist in leg strengthening.

your back with your arms on the ground along your sides, fold your legs into your chest with the soles of your feet turned upward. Two training partners, one on each leg, then lower their weight onto your legs, holding your upraised feet against their chests for stability. Using one leg at a time, push each training partner up into a standing position and then lower him back to the original pose. Repeat the exercise from leg to leg until you begin to tire.

Lower Torso Conditioning

Leg-pull sit-ups can be performed from a resting position flat on your back with your hands behind your head and your legs extended. Begin by concentrating on the long abdominal muscles that cover the front of the torso. Turn the concentration into gradual contraction and allow the body to flex and pull

inward, bringing the right elbow to the left knee with a release of the breath. Lower yourself back to the flattened position without resting your legs and then repeat the movement with your left elbow going to your right knee with a release of the breath. Return to the flat rest position and then repeat the right, left, and down routine eight more times. After completing nine repetitions, rest for a few moments and then do another set of nine. Continue until your body tells you that you are finished.

As another form of lower torso power conditioning, you can suspend yourself upside down from a crossbar or beam and perform the right-elbow-to-left-knee and left-elbow-to-right-knee routine for nine repetitions. Be sure that your legs are well engaged for total support and that you have a training partner working as a safety spotter for you before beginning this inverted curling exercise.

(Text continues on page 39.)

Leg-pull sit-ups build strength across the abdomen.

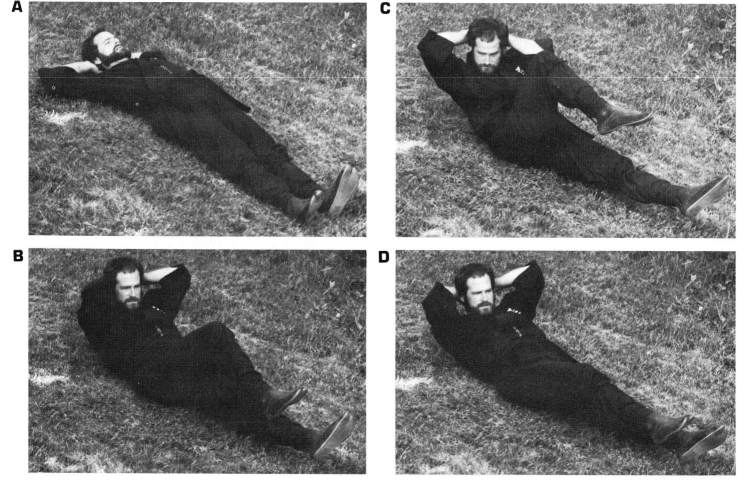

(Continued on next page.)

Using the hanging bar for torso strengthening.

E

F

G

H

A

B

(Continued on next page.)

C

D

E

F

Another variation of the abdominal curl exercise is to use the support of two training partners in order to create the means for inversion when no pole or beam is available. Hook the instep of each foot behind the necks of your two assistants and allow your body to drop into a suspended position. While your partners hold your legs in position, perform the same left and right elbow and knee routine as you would suspended from the bar, for a total of nine counts before resting.

B

A

Training partners can aid in torso curls for power and strength buildup.

C

(Continued on next page.)

D

E

F

G

Upper Torso Conditioning

The standard Western-style push-up position, with the hands just outside the shoulders, can be used to develop the muscles of the shoulders and upper arms. Rather than perform the rapid up-and-down push-up motion common to physical education classes and military PT sessions, however, a more thorough power-building exercise can be done by placing the hands farther apart, slowing down the action, and fully extending all muscles of the upper back and shoulders to the point of full flexion. On the way back down, lower yourself with a smooth and controlled glide rather than dropping and catching yourself at floor level. Though you may find yourself unable to do as many push-ups per session this way, the exercises you do perform will have a fuller intensity.

If appropriate equipment is available, the extended push-up exercise can be done with raised blocks or posts under the hands so that the arms are forced to flex even more as you go as far toward the ground as possible with your chest.

A

Extended push-ups take longer for each action and force the student to flex to total extension at the high point.

B

C

(Continued on next page.)

D

E

F

Raised blocks or posts make the extended push-up even more effective for total shoulder work.

A

(Continued on next page.)

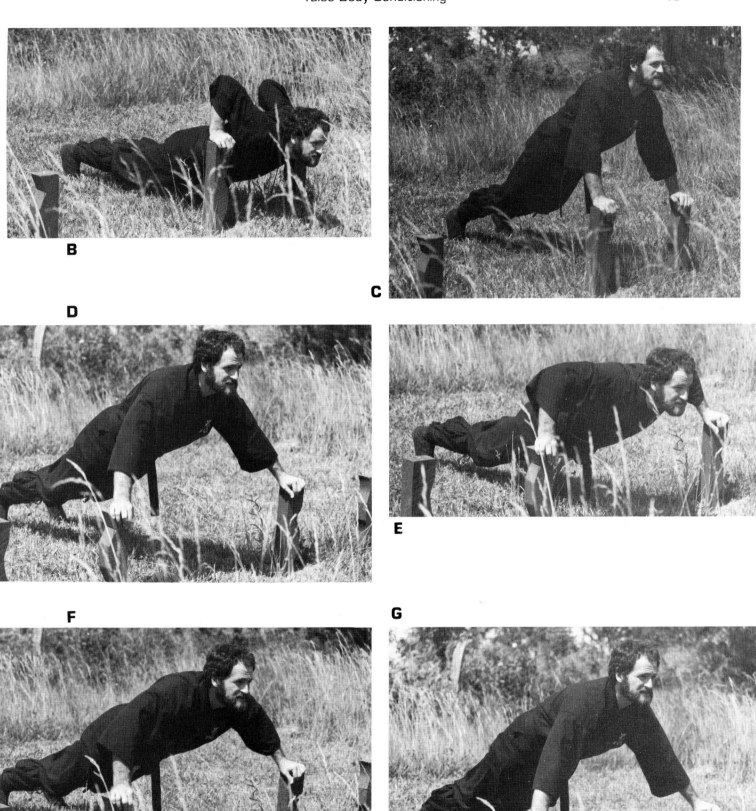

B

C

D

E

F

G

Another exercise for development of the upper torso is the hanging pull-up on a bar or beam, performed with the gripping hands at shoulder width or wider. As with the exaggerated push-up exercise, work for full extension and engagement of all of the upper torso and shoulder muscles. Do not merely jerk the body up to the bar and let it fall back to the relaxed position.

B

A

Hanging pull-ups with the arms spread wide work on the shoulders more than the arms.

C

Arm Conditioning

For increased arm power to deliver stronger punches and hits, execute more controlled throws, and handle a multitude of weapon types, the muscles of the arm can be exercised in ways that isolate and work the individual groups that require strengthening.

The upper arm can be exercised with a type of seated push-up. Using upright blocks, posts, or chair backs, extend your arms straight down and grip the tops of the supports. Slowly lower your hips as far as they will go by bending your arms. Flex the arms back to the straightened position to bring your body back up to the original height. Repeat the exercise until muscle fatigue sets in.

B

C

D

A

The seated push-up works the upper arms.

The forearms can be strengthened by doing underhanded cane rolling exercises. Grip one end of a three-foot *hanbo* cane with a reverse grip, allowing the cane to extend out from the base of the hand. Extend your arm with the elbow slightly bent and swing the cane in a repetitive horizontal figure-eight pattern. Bear in mind that twirling or swinging any weapon in a pattern is strictly a conditioning exercise and not a fighting technique.

A

B

Underhanded cane rolling in fig-ure-eight patterns works on the muscles of the forearms and grip-ping hands.

C

(Continued on next page.)

D

E

F

G

The entire arm can be exercised with a vertical suspended push-up. Use the support of two training partners to allow your body to remain head-down in the air while you perform the push-ups. Each training partner takes one leg and guides your body position so that the small of your back does not arch or bow. Use your arms alone to push yourself up slowly and lower yourself slowly, avoiding the tendency to bend your back so that more of your chest muscles come into play.

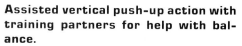

Assisted vertical push-up action with training partners for help with balance.

A

B

C

D

These exercises are just a few of the body conditioning methods appropriate for practitioners of *ninjutsu*. For the limited space available in an introductory volume of this nature, however, the foregoing conditioning methods provide an overview of the major muscle groups and some routines for power building that are applicable to each.

It should also be mentioned that, like the flexibility and suppleness training, power training is something that requires persistence and perseverance. A few brief attempts at these exercises will bring virtually no results. Power, like flexibility, is built up through long-term, programmed developmental work.

The use of free weights for building strength can be included in *ninjutsu* training. In general, it is suggested that lighter weights be used for larger numbers of repetitions, as opposed to heavier weights pushed for a few intense repetitions. In addition to accepted standard weightlifting routines as practiced the world over, specific results can be obtained by adapting the weights to an imitation of the combat action to be mastered for performance later on.

B

C

D

E

A

Light weights gripped in the hand assist in working the shoulder muscles that will deliver the upward and downward defensive strikes. The weight helps to discourage the weak habit of flexing the elbow, rather than rolling the shoulder, in an attempt at stopping power.

A

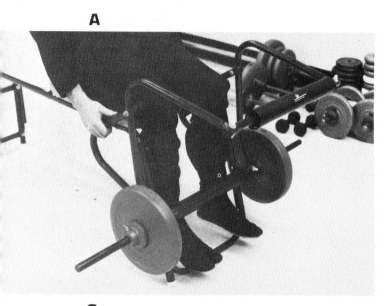

B

C

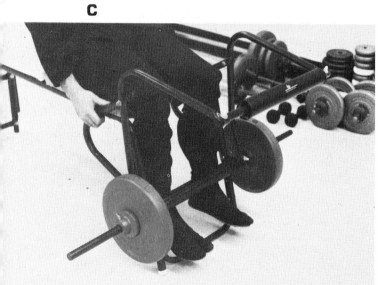

D

Westerners often have trouble developing the appropriate springy tension in the legs that aids in powerful punch and strike deliveries. Japanese students are conditioned all day long by continuously going up and down into the *seiza* kneeling posture. Western students can build up strength by using a weight set to perform leg flexes that will strengthen the small muscles in the knee joints.

A

B

C

Unique to the art of *ninjutsu* is the *shuriken* throwing star, which is used as a distracting weapon against pursuers. Here, a weight is used to simulate the flat blade in a horizontal throw, in order to encourage proper body dynamics. The most effective throwing method takes advantage of the body weight in motion, not flicking of the wrist, for propulsion. The weight in place of the blade tends to prevent flicking throws and teaches the student to be comfortable with the body's propelling the blade.

D

Aerobic Training

The legendary exploits of the historical ninja of Japan could have been possible only through the cultivation of the highest possible level of fitness in all aspects. The ability to run faster and farther or climb higher and longer than the average pursuer was a result of continuous conditioning training so that what was physically draining to the common man was accepted as routine for the ninja.

In this increasingly sedentary modern society a good aerobic workout becomes even more important. With the natural body movement that characterizes the ninja's *taijutsu* unarmed combat method, muscle tension and exertion are not a part of the action. Effective self-protection combat should not wear out the ninja, so combat training stresses the point of relaxing with the movements. Therefore, *dojo* training in self-protection methods should be supplemented with regular aerobic workouts at least three times per week.

After a sufficient warm-up of *taiso* stretching and muscle conditioning, you can use a 30-minute period of brisk walking or running as a start toward aerobic conditioning. Speed of movement is not important in the beginning. The key is to maintain a consistent level of exertion that causes the heartbeat to increase and the breathing rate and depth to intensify for at least 30 minutes at a time. As your body becomes used to the newfound fitness, you can increase your speed and intensity as you feel your capability growing.

4

TAIJUTSU
THE ART OF
USING THE BODY

The foundation of all aspects of the *ninjutsu* combat method is the practice and perfection of *nin-po taijutsu,* or the ninja's "art of using the body." *Taijutsu* is the original Japanese warrior method of unarmed combat, and its roots can be found far back in the history of Japan. As a system of life-or-death survival self-protection, as opposed to the modern martial arts more popular today, the ninja's *taijutsu* has to be able to cover all fighting possibilities. Without the luxury of rules, weight classifications, and skill level rankings, it is not possible to disallow or eliminate any potential technique or strategy that could be encountered in hand-to-hand combat.

Taijutsu is by nature a comprehensive method of employing the body's natural movements to avoid injury while dealing out the appropriate degree of injury to one's adversary. Obviously to anyone who has witnessed even a few actual street fights, this means that the ninja's unarmed combat method will have to provide ways of successfully subduing a boxer, a wrestler, a kicking expert, a karate or judo practitioner, a huge hulk, a weapon wielder, or multiple attackers, not to mention dogs or mechanical objects that could do one harm. Broad-based fighting skill is the key to surviv-

ing attacks on the street or in the field. The practitioner of an exclusive or specialized technique system will be in extreme danger when he discovers that he is in a situation for which his specialty is useless or less effective.

Some martial artists attempt to cover this combat weakness in the Zen moving meditation arts or the sports competition arts by synthesizing various elements into a hybrid combination of karate, *jujutsu, kung-fu,* boxing, stick fighting, and so on. Though these mismatched collections of unrelated components reflect an admirable attempt to deal with reality, those systems are doomed to produce mediocre results because there is no single set of principles that covers all methods of the multipart concoctions. Frustration and awkwardness will be encountered every time one part of the system is left for another part as the body and mind adjust to the shift in principles. This is, of course, no problem in a recreational martial art. But it is a deadly mistake in life-or-death confrontation.

The *taijutsu* approach uses the natural complementary relationships of size, mood, intensity, purpose, legality, speed, and weapon lethality in the fight to create the appropriate tactics in each situation. Sometimes we can be

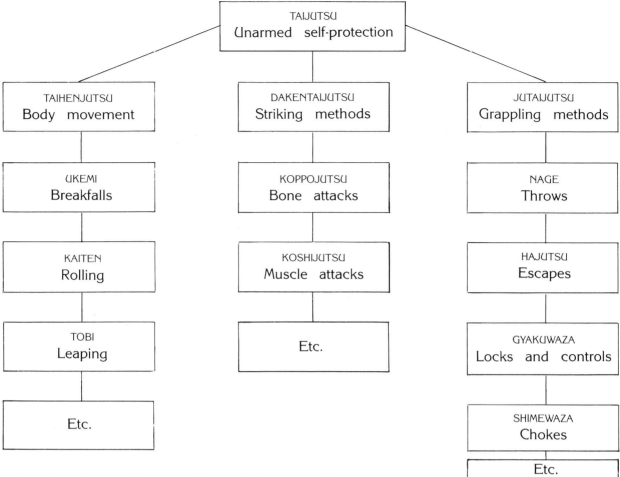

outnumbered; sometimes we face a faster or stronger adversary; sometimes we are armed with greater or lesser weapons. Any given confrontation is totally unique. *Nin-po taijutsu* is the method of taking those unique aspects, no matter what they are, and turning them into strengths that will bring victory.

Taijutsu is the overall description for the ninja's method of handling physical attacks. The art itself can be further examined structurally to better understand and describe how it works and how it is taught.

Of course, the ninja is not aware of those classifications when actually engaged in the second-to-second consciousness of self-protection combat. In that realm everything must be spontaneous, creative, and totally appropriate for the ever-changing reality found on the brink of life and death. The classification breakdown is of value only for purposes of explaining the training concepts to new students. In application *taijutsu* is one flowing experience of efficient body work that produces the needed results.

Footwork

Unlike many of the more popular martial arts, the ninja's *taijutsu* incorporates no "stances." This has been the case since its originator first began his study 800 years ago. Indeed, the idea of stances is relatively new to the warrior arts and is unfortunately one that is totally inappropriate for the action of realistic self-protection. The word *stance* implies something of a static nature; there is no way for you to stand there while another person is working at harming or killing you. The concept of footwork instead of stances is much more appropriate for the dynamic nature of personal combat.

The way your emotions, size, power, and intentions form relative strengths with those of your adversary will determine the most appropriate mode of footwork for the confrontation. As a general overview of possible footwork options, you can think of responding in one of four possible ways:

- **Stability**—you can hold your ground and

(Text continues on page 64.)

Stability in a fighting encounter is maintained by lowering the weight directly over the flexed knees. Example A shows a shift forward into the conflict.

Example B shows a drop of the weight in position by means of spreading the feet.

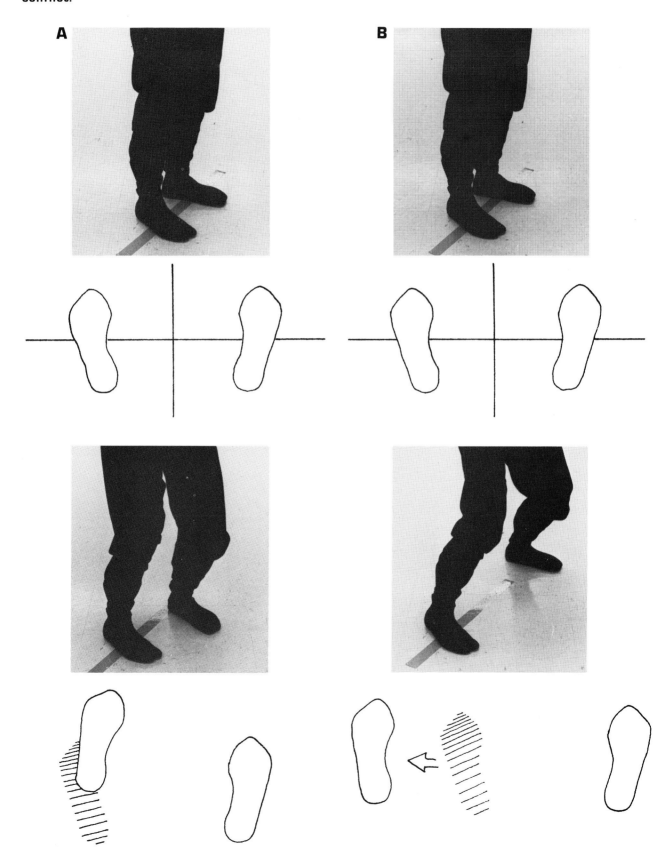

A

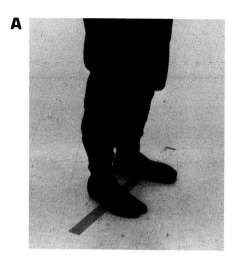

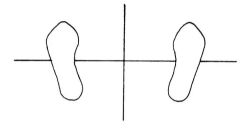

Defensiveness in a fighting encounter takes the ninja out of striking range with backpedaling footwork. Example A shows the first foot shift back.

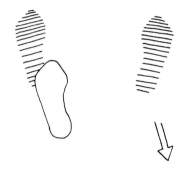

Example B shows another backpedaling shift, on the heels of the first.

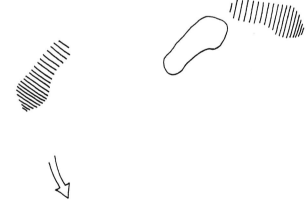

Example C shows a cross-step in the opposite
direction, angling away from the attacker's second move.

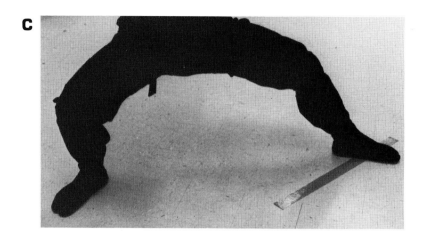

Aggressiveness is the quality of flying forward into the attack with a rear-foot push-off. Example A shows the initial forward move.

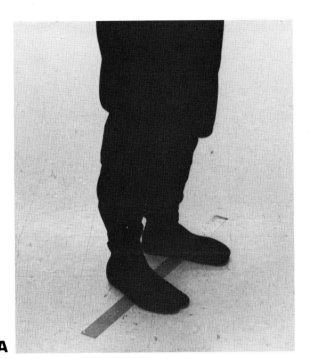

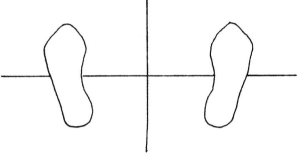

A

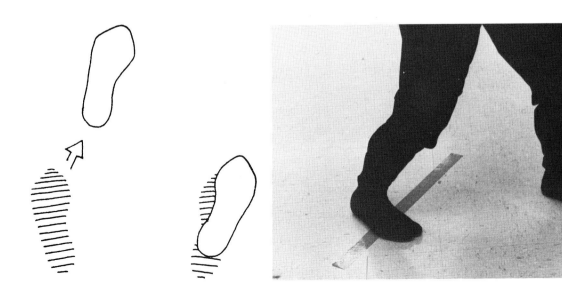

B

Example B shows a follow-up leading-leg shuffle.

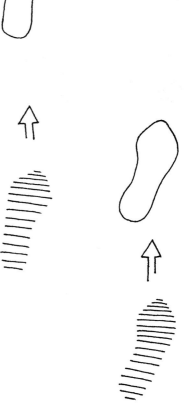

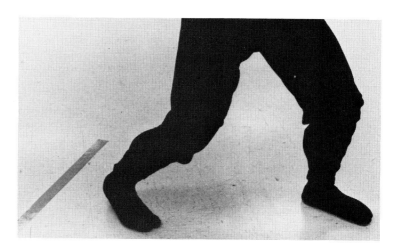

C

Example C shows a follow-up step-through lunge, in which the rear foot is thrown forward with the attack delivery.

Evasiveness in a fighting encounter is made possible by footwork that maneuvers the body into inaccessible positions. Example A shows a forward drifting step that goes around the attack.

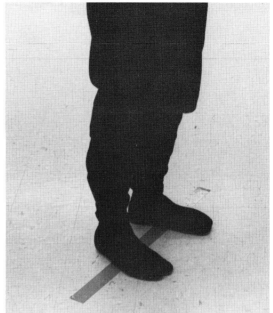

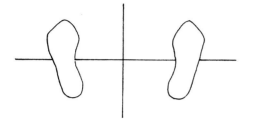

A

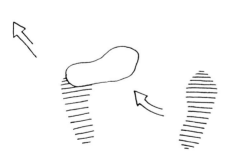

B

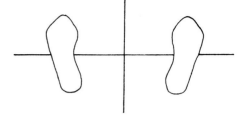

Example B shows a retreating foot shift that pulls the body out of the way of an attack.

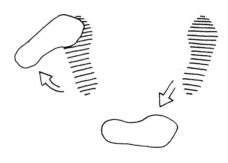

use immovable strength to defeat your enemy.

- **Defensiveness**—you can backpedal out of the clash and return with more appropriate angling to defeat your enemy.
- **Aggressiveness**—you can charge into the clash and overwhelm your enemy.
- **Evasiveness**—you can move in such a manner that your enemy cannot get to you as you take the fight to him.

There is also a fifth footwork method, in which the above elements are blended responsively to form what could be described as a **creative** pattern.

Natural Weapons

The use of the total body weapon is often overlooked by those martial arts that concentrate on a particular area of specialization. Kicking systems have no need of finger ripping attacks; boxing methods have no need of knee slam attacks; and judo training has no need of punching attacks, because all of these systems have been created around set rule structures. *Ninjutsu,* on the other hand, must operate as a ruleless method because of all the potential unbalanced situations that could be encountered in life-or-death confrontations.

As a guide for students new to the ninja combat method, the total body is seen as consisting of 16 weapons, or the *juroppoken* of *taijutsu.* The 16 fundamental weapons are:

Head	Left hand
Right shoulder	Right hip
Left shoulder	Left hip
Right elbow	Right knee
Left elbow	Left knee
Right hand	Right heel
Left heel	Left toes
Right toes	*taiken*

The 16th weapon is known as the *taiken,* or "body as weapon." This catchall number 16 includes all other less than primary weapons of the body, including the teeth, forearms, shins, ankles—anything that just happens to be in the right place to do some damage to an attacker.

When the natural weapons are applied against an adversary, the *ken tai ichi jo* principle of "body and weapon are one" makes the strike effective. In essence, the principle provides damaging or knockdown power by using the entire body motion and action to propel the weapon. Mere limb extension alone cannot generate the same degree of power.

In training, the student of *ninjutsu* is taught to move the feet, body, and weapon with a flowing action that creates simultaneity of step, movement, and strike. Caution and attention are strongly advised during the beginning phases of training, as that is where future habits are born. Those who tend to step, set the feet, and then punch will never break through to the sufficient speed of response necessary for combating a skilled attacker. Those who swing out with their punch and then allow the feet to shift after the blow will never break through to the power necessary for taking out a determined attacker. The key to efficient, effective movement is the coordinated, rhythmic engagement of the parts of the moving body, from ankles to fingertips, for total integration of energies, focus, and intention.

The following examples show some of the limitless variations possible with the fundamental natural weapons of the body. *Taijutsu* footwork principles, body dynamics concepts, and weapon applications work together in harmony to produce the needed results.

From a defensive posture, forward-driving, aggressive footwork carries the *shitoken* thumb drive strike into its target. Note that the body and arm move as one unit to provide power to the arm swing.

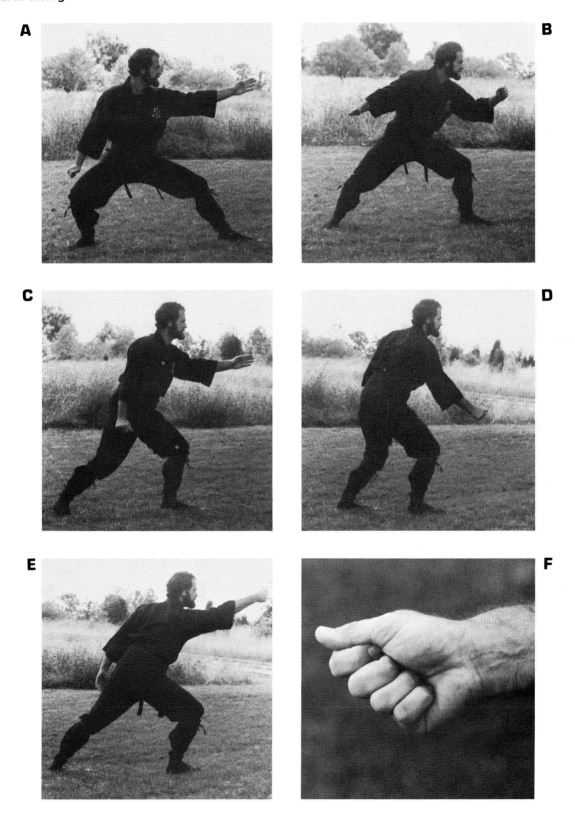

From an aggressive posture, the legs propel the *shikanken* extended-knuckle punch out toward its target. The knuckles extend just before impact to allow the fist additional reach as well as the capability to slip into tight target areas.

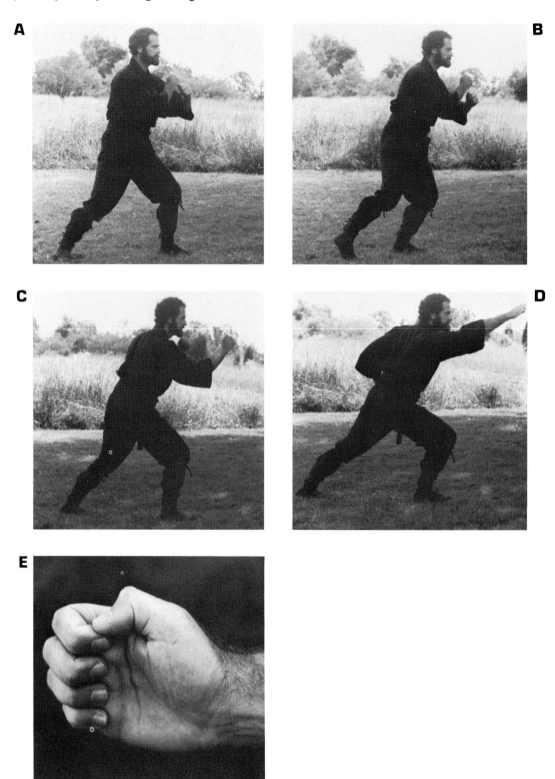

The *fudoken* clenched-fist strike is used here in an uppercutting punch application. The body moves with the swinging arm to increase the impact power over what could be generated by arm extension alone.

A

B

C

D

E

F

G

The *kitenken* hand-edge strike is used here in its *urashuto* application. In training, the students are taught to practice a large looping strike that allows for coordination of body and weapon in motion. The palm edge hits with a jarring slam and drives completely through the target. It does not merely flex and return with a stinging slap action.

D

A

E

B

F

C

G

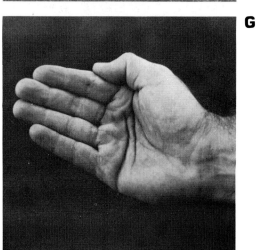

Again, the ninja's *taijutsu kitenken* hand-edge strike is applied with forward-charging footwork. In this application, however, the striking action is the *omoteshuto* attack to an imaginary adversary's neck.

From a defensive posture, the hips are rocked forward to initiate the attacking motion, and the rear leg is folded and then flexed to slam the *sokuyaku* sole of the foot out as a *zempogeri* forward kick.

A

B

C

D

The *sokuyaku* foot-stamp kick is applied here in a *sokuhogeri* sideways kick toward an imaginary adversary to the side.

A

B

C

The leading leg is pulled back into the *hicho no kamae* single-leg defensive posture to clear an adversary's leg attack. From the coiled position, the leg is immediately shoved forward in a *sokuyaku* heel-stamp kick.

A

B

C

D

E

F

The bottom of the heel is used here in a *kohogeri* back-kicking application against an adversary approaching from the rear. The body is lowered into the kick by flexing the ground support leg for increased stability.

From the ninja's *kosei no kamae* attacking posture, the rear leg is lifted and shoved forward in a *kakushigeri* "hidden kick" application. In a clash with an adversary, the kick can be sent out into its target without being seen.

A

B

C

D

From the *ichimonji no kamae* defensive posture of *taijutsu* unarmed combat, the leading arm is rolled inward and down to create a lower-level defensive counterstrike against an incoming kick or punch to the lower body. As the rolling strike is executed, the rear foot shuffles out and away from the danger zone with simultaneous body angling.

An upper-level defensive counterstrike is executed from the *dokko no kamae* defensive posture as the rear leg is shifted to the rear and side to create the proper range. The *fudoken* clenched fist strikes the adversary's incoming arm or leg with a damaging strike in response to the attack. The move is not so much a block as a counterattack into the moving weapon.

A

B

C

D

E

Ground-Hitting Skills

The concept of self-protection reaches far beyond the limits of mere fistfights in total scope. Protection skills could also cover escaping from burning buildings, tumbling down staircases, or surviving automobile crashes. The *taihenjutsu* "body changing arts" of the *ninjutsu* combat method emphasize the importance of ground-hitting techniques for safety and for extra assurance that the student can survive any life-or-death confrontation.

Rolling methods take the ninja to the ground in a way that allows for escape while permitting him or her to regain footing as a part of the action. Whether thrown to the ground, knocked down, or willfully dropping in escape, the ninja is conditioned to use the ground as an ally. Relax into the roll naturally, allow the breath to fall from the lungs without a tense blast, and curl the body with the motion of the action. Do not "work at" the roll. Use the pull of gravity to take you down and over in a natural tumble.

Training in the Fundamentals

The goal of *taijutsu* training is free and responsive fluidity that allows the ninja warrior always to be in the right position, always to be in control of the action, and always to be out of the way of the enemy's potentially harmful actions. Obviously, such spontaneous adaptability cannot be memorized for a later date; it must be a product of the current moment. There are, however, exercises that practitioners new to the art can repeat to get a fuller grounding in the adaptability and governability of the body in combat. The *kihon gata* fundamentals are seen as models, or foundations, upon which spontaneous decision making is later based.

For effective training, any part of the total combat action can be selected, isolated, and improved upon through drill, exploration of effects, and internalization of essence. By working individual pieces of the total skill desired, eventual mastery is gained through systematic progression. The student could choose to focus training attention on considerations of footwork, power delivery, reaction timing, creative response, or any other aspect that seems to be holding the student back.

As a general guide, unarmed or weapon combat skill capabilities can be practiced through four major training focus methods, which follow.

Shadowboxing

The student can practice any given movement or technique series in solo fashion to better understand and capture the purpose and essence of the action. This method is the repetitive drill that is usually considered self-developmental homework for the student and is rarely relied upon as a training hall learning device.

Sparring

Work with a training partner for technique reaction drills is of major importance in *taijutsu* training. Through simulated fighting clash encounters with fellow training hall members, students can experience the elements of proper distancing, timing, tension and relaxation, perception, and creative awareness. Work with training partners makes up the bulk of *dojo* workout sessions, with selected aspects of shadowboxing and target impact work occasionally included to balance out the group learning experience.

Target Hitting

The student must practice the fundamental techniques of the ninja combat method against a variety of realistic targets. While shadowboxing work and sparring drills are important for developing a consciousness of body movement as the primary source of power, mobility, and evasiveness, target work is crucial for learning to deliver the effects of the weapon in motion. Hanging body bags, hand-held mitts or foam shields, suspended ropes, and log posts are a few of the targets that must be engaged

(Text continues on page 84.)

The *zempokaiten* forward roll can be used to escape from pressure that forces you forward or straight down to the ground. The body curls with the forward motion and rocks over along the spine to bring you up on your feet again.

Kohokaiten rear rolling is a mirror image of the forward roll action; the sequence is reversed to accommodate rearward pressure that forces you back and down. The body drops back and down to allow the legs to curl over the shoulders, taking the feet into position on the ground behind you.

(Continued on next page.)

Right and left *sokuhokaiten* sideways rolling is used to escape from certain throws, striking attempts, and assaults that demand a lateral evasion. The body drops over and out to the side to generate a rolling action that crosses the back just below the shoulder blades and brings you back to your feet again.

A   B   C

D   E   F

(Continued on next page.)

Shoulder rolling takes the body forward or rearward diagonally to move away from danger. The action rolls across the back from right shoulder to left hip, or from left shoulder to right hip in the forward version, taking you out to the side and forward at the same time. The rear version of the roll has action that goes from right hip to left shoulder, or from left hip to right shoulder, taking you out to the side and backward at the same time.

(Continued on next page.)

G

H

I

J

K

L

over and over again in order to develop truly reliable stopping power and shock effect in one's punches, strikes, and kicks. Like shadowboxing, however, target work is suggested as homework for self-development rather than as the major thrust for training hall group workouts.

Visualization

Practice in proper mind-set, awareness, and consciousness direction is the fourth major aspect of the ninja's *taijutsu* combat training. Though not as obvious to beginning students of *ninjutsu* as the more overtly physical requirements of the training, the mental powers must ultimately be developed if the overall training program is to be successful. Skills of visualization can be used to enhance the assimilation of new movement principles and fundamental techniques, and mind-set alteration is the key to creating artificially the pressures of life-or-death realism even though one is in the safety of the training hall in actuality.

Footwork Drills

The various means of effectively moving the body into or away from an attack can be isolated and practiced to better understand the roles of mobility, distancing, and rhythms in a clash. The footwork drills are usually accompanied by some elementary actions with the upper body weapons, but the drills are not intended literally to recreate a fighting situation. The training partners limit themselves to the action to be practiced and assist each other in attaining the essence of the drill. Each person repeats the action series over and over again to reinforce the internalization of the concepts being pursued.

Creating footwork drills is a simple process. During normal training in the *dojo* you will encounter trouble areas in which your body does not seem to be able to do what you want it to do. Eliminate all of the pressures of performing the technique as a realistic clash, streamline or remove any complex or multipart response actions, and allow yourself to experience the essence of the footwork you need in a slow-motion repetition of the fundamentals.

The following examples are offered as suggestions of how to approach the mastery of *taijutsu* fundamental footwork strengths. These drills are intended to lead to eventual overall proficiency and are purposely designed not to be realistic self-protection scenarios.

A  **B**

Defensive backpedaling footwork is practiced in this drill. The simulated attacker continues after the defender with a series of realistic lunging punches to the face. The training partner taking the defensive role in the drill shifts back and to the inside of each punch to apply a counterpunch into the attacker's exposed wrist every time he advances with a punch.

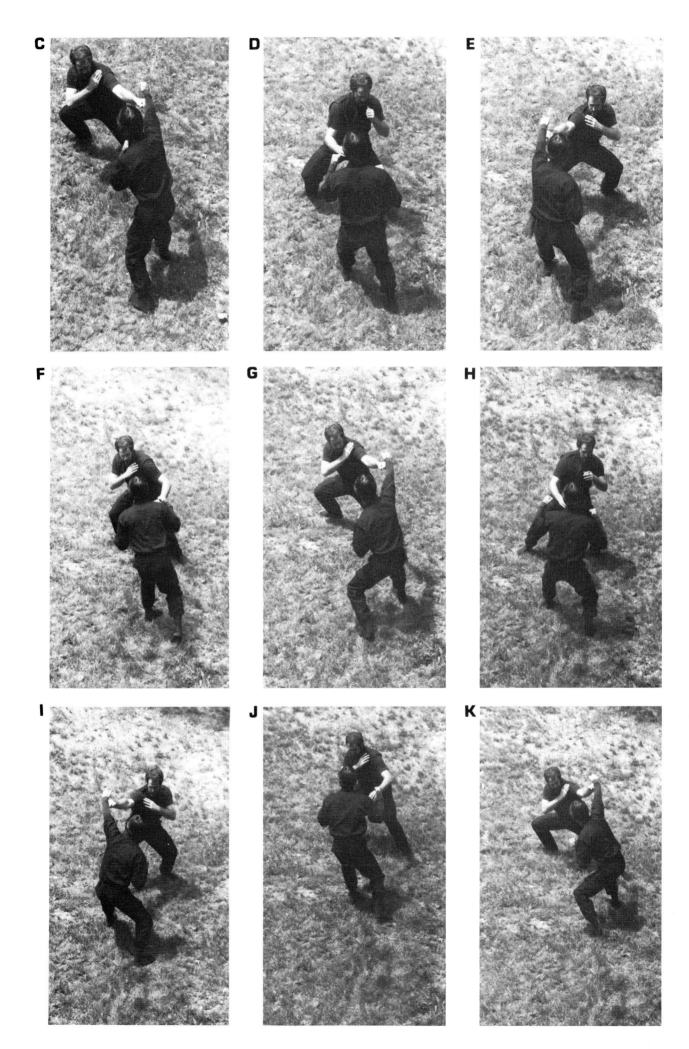

Another application of defensive backpedaling is practiced in this drill. The attacking training partner goes after the defending partner with a series of straight lunging punches to the face. The defender shifts back and to the outside of each punch to apply a counterpunch into the outside of the attacker's exposed forearm or wrist every time he executes a punch at the defender. The drill can continue for any number of punches.

A

B

C

(Continued on next page.)

Wavelike defense and counter footwork is demonstrated in this training example. The defensive action becomes a countering punch or kick, which is interpreted as a new attack by each training partner over and over again. Attacking and defending students trade roles with each exchange until nine full repetitions of the exercise are completed. The object is to use effective distancing and angling to get as far out of range as possible and then move back into range with a realistic counterattack at the training partner.

A

B

C

D

E

(Continued on next page.)

Reaction Drills

Crucial to developing a feeling of confidence and mastery in a self-protection encounter is the acknowledged sense of "having been there before," no matter what comes along. Repeated exposure to and experience in handling dangerous situations create a feeling of self-assured control, through the process of gradual desensitization. If one sees something shocking over and over again, that thing eventually loses its shock value and becomes commonplace. Remember what you went through in order to overcome the initial fears of driving a car on the open road, of leaping off a high diving board, or of getting up to speak before a large audience of strangers. The same effect of confidence as a product of repeated exposure is possible through realistic training in the combat arts.

The following training drills show some examples of the ninja's *taijutsu* in action against simulated attackers. Students and teachers alike work to inject a feeling of realism and urgency into the exchanges. Stylized movements, limited ranges of actions, and lack of natural physiological response to the initial damaging hit must all be avoided in combat self-defense training, as these are the training hall bad habits that will prevent one from handling any and all possible violent encounters on the street or in the field. The reaction drills incorporate all aspects of *taijutsu*, from strikes to throws to escapes. Attacker and defender roles can be assigned, as can specific attack and defense actions, or the exercise can take a freer, more spontaneous form that allows for the elements of surprise and strategy in advanced training.

In this *taijutsu* reaction drill the defending student backpedals away to the outside of the attacker's advancing punch. The injurious strike to the attacker's wrist is immediately followed up with a heel-stamp kick to the ribs as a means of unbalancing the attacker and knocking him down.

A

B

The potential number of reaction drills is limitless, as all sorts of potential street and field attacks can be practiced. In this example of *taijutsu* reaction training the defender backpedals away to the inside of the attacker's advancing punch. As soon as the attacker's wrist has been hit with the defender's counterblow, the defender shifts his hips forward to propel his body and *shikanken* extended-knuckle punch into the attacker's throat before the attacker has a chance to complete his second punch.

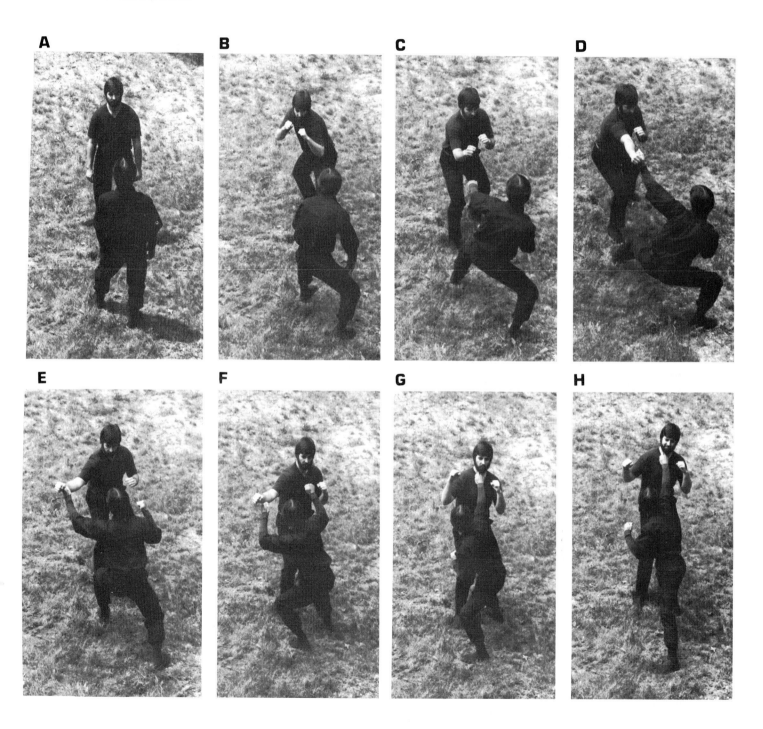

A   B   C   D

E   F   G   H

The defending student charges into his adversary's technique in this reaction drill against a grab and punch. The defender secures the attacker's grabbing arm in an *onikudaki* elbow-leverage application and swings his body around behind the attacker to avoid a possible hit or grab from the attacker's free hand. The defender then kicks the attacker's leg out from beneath him to take him to the ground.

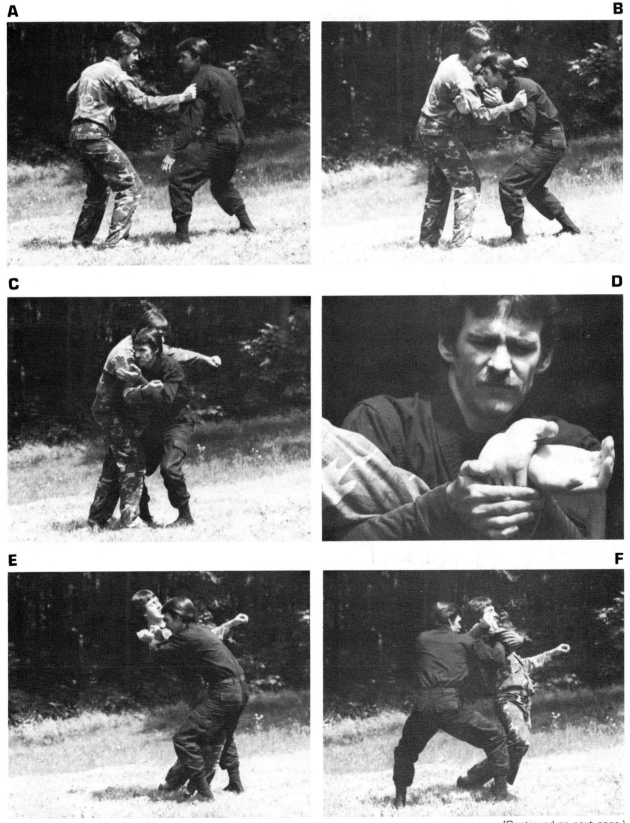

A

B

C

D

E

F

(Continued on next page.)

G

H

I

J

In this *taijutsu* drill the defender evades the attacker's punch by moving to the outside of the grabbing arm while applying elbow jamming pressure on the outside of the wrist. The defending student then knocks the attacker's hand free and stuns his adversary with an elbow to the face. From there the defender backpedals to sling his simulated foe onto the ground with an *omotegyaku* outward wrist twist.

Against this grab-and-punch attack, the defender pulls back and executes a defensive strike against the incoming punch. An eye jab immediately follows to throw off the attacker's timing. The attacking student's grabbing hand is then ripped from its hold, and the defender uses backstepping footwork and an *uragyaku* inward wrist twist to force his adversary to the ground in submission.

A

B

C

D

(Continued on next page.)

E

F

G

H

In this *taijutsu* reaction drill the defender uses the attacker's pulling motion to set him up for an *osotonage* rear hip throw. Once the defender realizes that resistance will not permit escape, he moves forward into the attacker's body and jams his leading hip into the attacker's hip to topple him. Note that the defender uses his torso in balanced motion, not a flex or forward bend at the hips, to throw his attacker to the ground.

The defender goes with the attacker's initial resistance to apply a *gansekinage* forward hip throw in this reaction drill training example. The defender uses his body in a lateral pivot, not a forward bending motion, to sling his attacker to the ground.

In this example the defender evades the effects of the *onikudaki* shoulder dislocation by going with the force of the larger attacker. Tension in the shoulder being attacked provides the lift to accompany the spring of the feet that takes the defender up and around to position for a stamp kick counter.

A

B

C

D

(Continued on next page.)

E

F

G

H

The defender uses his height to advantage in this escape example. Moving under the attacker's lunge, the defender uses his body weight in motion to create the power for a shoulder slam to the ribs, followed by a diving roll against the locked knee. After breaking the knee joint, the defender continues with his forward roll to turn it into a heel-stamp kick against the downed attacker.

(Continued on next page.)

To escape from an *uragyaku* inward wrist-breaking technique, the defender allows himself to go with the attacker's power and momentum. The defender turns the throw into a diagonal shoulder roll, which brings him back toward his adversary unexpectedly. A kick from the ground stuns the attacker, who is then taken to the ground in a reversal of the wrist twist.

A

B

C

D

E

F

G

The defender avoids the attacker's grab and punch by charging into the attack with a *fudo-ken* hammering fist to the attacker's biceps. Rather than contend with the attacker's grip on his trailing arm, the defender continues the motion of his leading arm and converts his strike into a flying version of the *mushadori* elbow leverage. Upon landing on his feet after damaging the attacker's elbow joint, the defender uses his hip to slam into the attacker's extended leg. The weight in motion forces the attacker to the ground. If the attacker still maintains a grip on the defender and tries to pull him down, the defender rolls backward to apply an arm bar lock on the attacker's injured arm.

(Continued on next page.)

To escape from the attacker's jacket grab, the defender leaps up to slam his knees into the attacker's crotch. The defender then uses his dropping body weight to pull the attacker forward onto his head with a neck-breaking strike and follows up with a rolling action that turns into a knee dislocation.

To counter the attacker's *omotegyaku* outward wrist-breaking technique, the defender allows himself to roll backward across his hip as a means of escaping the effects of the technique. The defender then rises to a kneeling position, where he has reversed the wrist twist and from which he leans forward in a *kumi-uchi*-style leg leverage that forces the attacker to the ground.

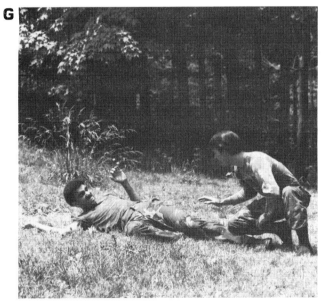

5
NINJA WEAPONS FOR COMBAT

Because of the self-protection combat orientation of the art of *ninjutsu,* work with weapons is a skill area of major importance in training sessions. Since the ninja's combat method is totally integrated and comprehensive in nature and not a mere collection of separate disciplines, *taijutsu* body movement principles form the base for work with all ninja weapon systems. The very same body actions that carry a leading-hand strike to the adversary also take the knife to its target. Identical footwork is used when applying an unarmed shoulder-dislocating lock and an ensnaring bind with the short chain weapon. Knockdown power for both a heel-stamp kick and a long staff ramming strike is generated with exactly the same body dynamics. In the *Bujinkan dojo* approach to warrior training, it can honestly be said that to learn to use a knife is to learn to punch, which is to learn to strike with the 12-foot chain. Any one piece is but a part of the greater whole.

As a general overview of weapon training classifications, it could be noted that the primary weapon type groupings are:

Stick Weapons
Canes   Clubs
Staffs   Poles

Blade Weapons
Knives   Daggers
Swords   Machetes

Flexible Weapons
Chains   Cords
Ropes

Projectile Weapons
Throwing blades   Firearms
Arrows   Blowguns
Grenades

Specialty Weapons
Battlefield poleaxes   Canes with
Rope and dagger   concealed chains
   weapons   Etc.

Training in the ninja *dojo* is geared toward familiarity with effective principles for each weapon group, rather than set techniques for specific weapons. With training in principles, the practitioner is not limited to one standard weapon, but can pick up anything and successfully press it into use for personal defense.

Historically, the most frequently encountered weapons for ninja of the feudal ages in Japan were the sword, spear, and bow and arrow. Training through apprenticeship fo-

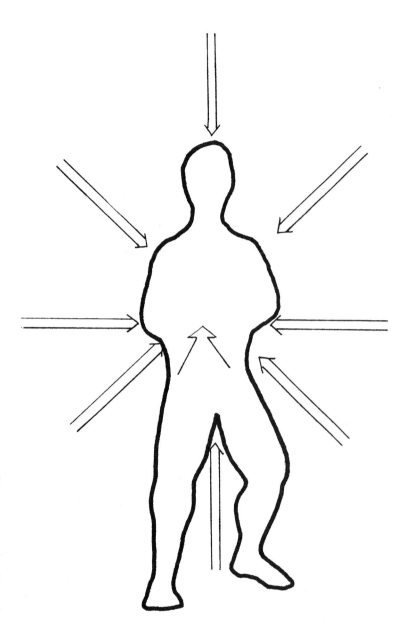

Strikes in nine directions can be employed when using the universal crosspalm grip.

cused heavily on the use of and countermeasures against those three weapons, because that is where the maximum danger and greatest potential deadliness was to be found. Unique tactics for disarming attackers bearing the standard three weapons were developed, along with special weapons that had characteristics designed to overcome any advantages the enemy's weapon might afford him in confrontation.

For guidance in *ninjutsu* training today, it is important to focus on the meaning behind the actual training drills of 500 years ago. Instruction and training emphasis dealt with the deadliest and most frequently encountered weapons of the day. If we apply these criteria to life in our day, we find that weapons like knives, crowbars, and handguns have replaced their ancient cousins in potential deadliness for practitioners of the art today. Therefore, in keeping with the tradition of the centuries-old art, most *ninjutsu* weapon training emphasis today is placed on contemporary street-lethal weapons that are readily available for use in self-protection and are highly likely to be encountered in violent confrontations.

Weapon Grips

The weapon, whether blade, stick, or chain, should be held in a manner that permits the fullest possible range of movement, reach, and flexibility. A diagonal crosspalm grip is the fundamental method of holding all weapons for use in self-protection combat. This permits the weapon to work as a natural extension of the moving arm in a fight, so that learning special body actions is unnecessary.

The universal crosspalm grip allows for total freedom and applicability in the striking trajectory of the weapon in hand. An imaginary grid of nine directional hits can be held in mind during target work and simulated clash sparring. Horizontal, vertical, diagonal, and lunging hits are all possible options with the weapon when a proper grip is employed.

The *hanbo* is gripped across the palm so that it forms an extension of the arm when the wrist is held in a natural position. Whether the staff is gripped in a forward or reverse manner, the hand is still able to flex and strike with natural dynamics.

A

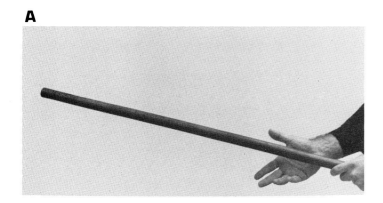

B

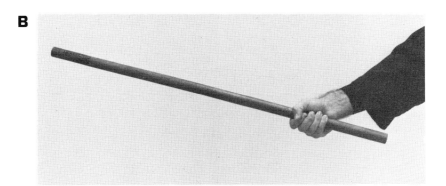

C

The knife is gripped across the palm, following the line of the extended thumb. The gripping hand folds naturally around the handle with an extended feel as the result in either the forward or the reverse grip. Do not grab the handle with a hammer grip that positions the blade at a 90-degree angle to the wrist.

A

C
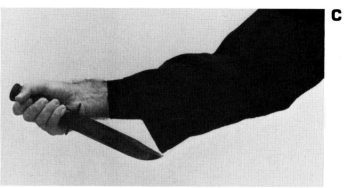

B

As with all other weapons, the *kusarifundo* short chain weapon is gripped across the palm for ease of natural extension. Prior to combat application, or as a means of making close-range damaging strikes, the chain can be gripped with the weights concealed by the folded fingers.

A

B
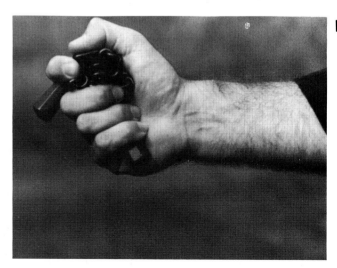

As with the short blade, the sword is gripped to provide a natural extension of the reach for cutting. The two-handed grip is used for leverage and stability in the forward position, and the free arm is used for support and guidance with the reverse grip.

A

B

C

Footwork

The inclusion of a weapon or weapons in a fight does not change the quality of the ninja's *taijutsu* body dynamics principles. A fight is a fight, whether the action is predominantly grappling, knife slashing, or bullet trading. Terms like *stick fighting, fistfighting,* and *sword fighting* are in a way misleading to the student, as they tend to draw too much attention to the weapon and thereby limit the fighter's options. Kicks seem more appropriate in a clash where both combatants hold knives, if we do not refer to the confrontation as a knife fight. Choking forearm takedowns seem more appropriate in a clash where one combatant has a club and the other has a cane, if we do not refer to the clash as a stick fight.

Refer again to the footwork diagrams and examples that appear in the preceding chapter on *taijutsu.* The four types of body dynamics (stability, defensiveness, aggressiveness, and evasiveness) are equally applicable to combat with weapons, and the footwork mechanics are identical.

The aggressive forward-springing footwork used to propel a horizontal knife cut into its target is identical to that used to send the leading-hand punch into its target. Footwork and body dynamics are the same. Only the weapon is different.

A

B

C

In this footwork example, defensive backpedaling takes the body out of dangerous range while the leading arm applies a damaging counter. With identical body action, both the *hanbo* cane and the *fudoken* clenched fist sail into an attacking limb with an angular strike.

A

B

C

D

Lunging, aggressive footwork takes the *zem-pogeri* front heel-stamp kick as well as the tip of the *rokushakubo* long staff into their respective targets. In both cases the fighters begin their strikes just as their bodies begin to move. One uses a foot and the other uses a wooden staff, however. With this type of efficient movement, the body mass in motion, not the limb alone, drives the weapon into its target.

Evasive circular motion is the key to effective swinging kicks and strikes with the concealed iron ring end of the *kyoketsu shoge* ring, cord, and hooked dagger weapon. By pivoting the body core from the knees up, the slinging motion is created and directed out to the weapon, providing power whether the weapon is a foot, an iron ring, a knife, or a fist. The weapon and body then move as one unit.

A

B

C

D

E

F

Wavelike defensive footwork that immediately turns into forward-surging, aggressive movement is shown here as the means for propelling both a looping uppercut punch and a circular *ninja gatana* sword slash into their respective targets. The lift and forward-moving action of the body in motion sends the weapons up and into their paths.

A

B

C

D

Evasive footwork is epitomized by short-chain striking methods that utilize circular stepping patterns and body turns. The limb and body move together so that the body in motion, rather than the flailing limb, actually provides the impact. This mode of body dynamics also prevents the weighted end of the chain from rebounding off the target and coming back at the weapon handler.

A

B

C

D

(Continued on next page.)

E   F

G   H

I   J

(Continued on next page.)

K L

M N

Fundamental Training Exercises

Just as the *taijutsu* unarmed combat training can be subclassified into components of striking, ground hitting, joint lock escapes, and the like, weapon application training can also be seen in terms of skill development areas. Regardless of weapon or type, fully developed proficiency will cover all of the following considerations for combat application.

Primary Application Skills

The fundamentals of applying the effects of the weapon are practiced in shadowboxing drills, simulated-clash sparring sessions, and actual target-striking work. The basics of weapon use are stressed, with no reference to advanced or complex counters. The primary nine cuts with a knife, the nine directional hits with a *hanbo* cane, the nine directional whipping strikes with the short weighted chain, and basic firearms aim and fire techniques are examples of the primary skills that must first be learned before going into advanced application work. There is no use in learning intricate knife timing drills if you cannot even properly cut a stationary target.

Defensive Counter Techniques

The principles of using the weapon in a fight against other similar or different weapons are taught through set examples of typical fighting clashes, bearing in mind the realistic damaging effects of the weapon as it connects with its target. In this area of training the students work knife against knife, stick against stick, chain against blade, staff against chain, and all possible combinations of weapon selection that could be encountered on the street or in the field. Timing, rhythm, distancing, strategy, and the "breath" of the fight are stressed through drill routines and simulated fighting clashes.

Weapon Disarms

The skills of gaining control of the adversary's weapon and taking it away from him or turning it against him are learned through adapted *taijutsu* combat drills, techniques, and strategies. The student can work unarmed against a weapon for training in realistic unarmed defense against a killing attack, or he or she can work with one weapon against another for training in the ability to moderate the degree of severity needed to subdue an armed attacker.

Weapon Retention

The skills and perceptions needed to retain control of one's own weapon when an adversary is working to take that weapon away are learned through adaptations of the weapon disarm techniques and drills. Students train by deliberately placing themselves in fighting scenarios and situations in which their simulated techniques have failed or their weapons have been grabbed by a training partner. From these purposely compromised situations in the training hall, the students can learn to apply spontaneous and creative responses in life-threatening combat clashes.

Specialty Aspects

Unique aspects of certain weapons, or special-use requirements for certain situations, are taught along with the four standard weapon skill considerations for full proficiency. Some of these specialties are sword or pistol fast-draw abilities, knife-throwing skills, firearm cover and concealment principles, and climbing methods that use the *kyoketsu shoge* cord and hooked dagger weapon of the historical Japanese ninja.

A

The defender moves with evasive circular action to avoid the attacker's knife slash while positioning himself to make an effective counter. Once inside the attack, the defender slams the end of his knife handle into the attacker's moving arm to stop him. The move is an attack, and not a blocking action. Once the arm has been hit, the attacker can then reach up and seize the attacker's knife wrist. The speed of the attack will prevent the defender from grabbing first and hitting second. The defender then shifts his body weight to send a strike to the attacker's temple and can next pull the blade edge down across the side of the attacker's neck if it is necessary to protect the defender's life.

B

C

D

E

In this knife-against-knife struggle the defender sends his blade hand over the attacking stab of his adversary to strike him in the upper ribs with the end of the handle, rather than cut him with the blade. The defender's knife then loops behind the attacker's elbow as the attacker attempts to free himself with a twisting flail. The defender secures the attacker's other arm and disarms him without having to cut or kill the attacker.

A

B

C

D

(Continued on next page.)

E

F

G

In this example of *ninjutsu* weapons in action the defender backpedals defensively with a rising counterslash to the attacker's initial cut, allowing her blade edge to pull along the underside of the attacker's wrist. When the attacker continues with another cutting attempt, the defender charges forward with a second cut to the same attacking arm and then follows with a piercing cut to the attacker's throat.

A

B

C

D

(Continued on next page.)

E

F

G

The attacker moves forward menacingly with several slashing cuts to create a feeling of uncertainty in the defender. Rather than attempt to engage the erratically moving blade with his own knife, however, the defender throws his foot up and around into the side of the attacker's arm as it brings the blade forward within range. Immediately, the defender shifts forward with a counterattack, directing his knife at the attacker's midsection. The defender then uses a knee-slam strike to the handle end of the knife to drive the blade into the target while simultaneously trapping the attacker's knife wrist with his thigh and hip. The knee-strike leg is then redirected downward with a heel-stamp kick to the attacker's knee, taking him to the ground. It is important to note that the defender maintains control of the attacker's knife throughout the fight, once he gains control.

(Continued on next page.)

The defender responds to the attacker's midsection slash with an evasive countercut that redirects the attacker's stab upward and away from its intended target. This counter is an aggressive cutting action, not a mild parry. Following the action of the weapon redirection, the defender sends her *fudoken* forefist smash into the underside of the attacking arm, stunning the attacker and perhaps even knocking the blade from his grip. From there, the defender drops her knife to hip level and, with a twisting body action, stabs into the attacker's lower abdomen. The bone structure of the defender's own hip is used to give the blade thrust additional power by pressing in on the end of the handle. As the attacker tumbles back and down, the defender grips her knife so that it is not pulled from her hand by the attacker's falling body.

A

B

C

D

(Continued on next page.)

The attacker moves in with a downward stabbing action. The defender uses his own stability and a forearm slam to knock the attacker's blade from its target. The defender then redirects his forearm into a slam against the attacker's face, before pulling him back into a throat-crushing forearm choke. Note that the defender has moved into position totally behind the attacker in order to avoid a possible stab or arm throw counter.

The attacker holds the defender at gunpoint and moves in to take the weapon from his holster. With smooth and sudden action, the defender shifts forward outside of the attacker's gun arm. He simultaneously gains control of the attacker's pistol while executing a close-range elbow strike to the attacker's jaw. Note that the escape move is a body advance, not a stationary pivot. The defender then uses knee leverage to down his adversary. Twisting pressure into the downed attacker's wrist and a crushing heel stamp onto the inner side of the attacker's shin free the pistol from his grip.

The attacker reaches out and grabs the defender's pistol and attempts to force it down and take it away. Rather than attempt to outmuscle his attacker, the defender drops to position himself and then uses his legs to rise into a jamming counter into the attacker's wrist. With a jarring completion of the wrist roll, the defender frees himself from the attacker's grip, successfully retaining his own weapon.

A

B

C

D

(Continued on next page.)

E

 F

G

Proper *taijutsu* body movement is the key to the lifesaving techniques of *ninjutsu*. In this example the defender drops back to the outside of his adversary's gun arm. By moving backward with a body pivot as the attacker pushes forward, the defender can clear the muzzle of the weapon. Note that this is *not* the dangerously deficient spin-around usually taught by instructors who do not know any better. The entire body drops out of the firing line with the *taijutsu* method. The defender then slams the attacker face-first into the automobile body and executes a knee slam to the base of the spine to set the attacker up for a sling to the ground. The attacker's trigger finger can be broken backward if necessary to get the pistol out of his hand. The defender then uses a *kohogeri* back kick to get the attacker away from him before turning the commandeered pistol on the occupants of the waiting automobile. Under actual street circumstances, the entire episode would have transpired in less than six seconds.

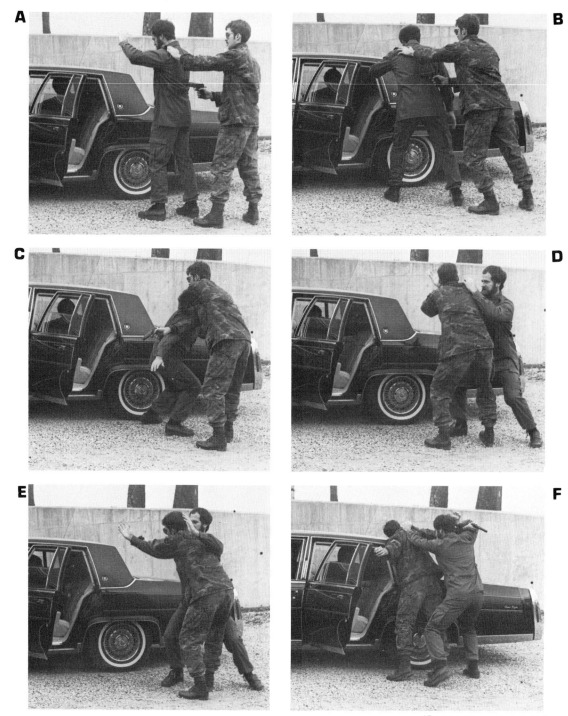

(Continued on next page.)

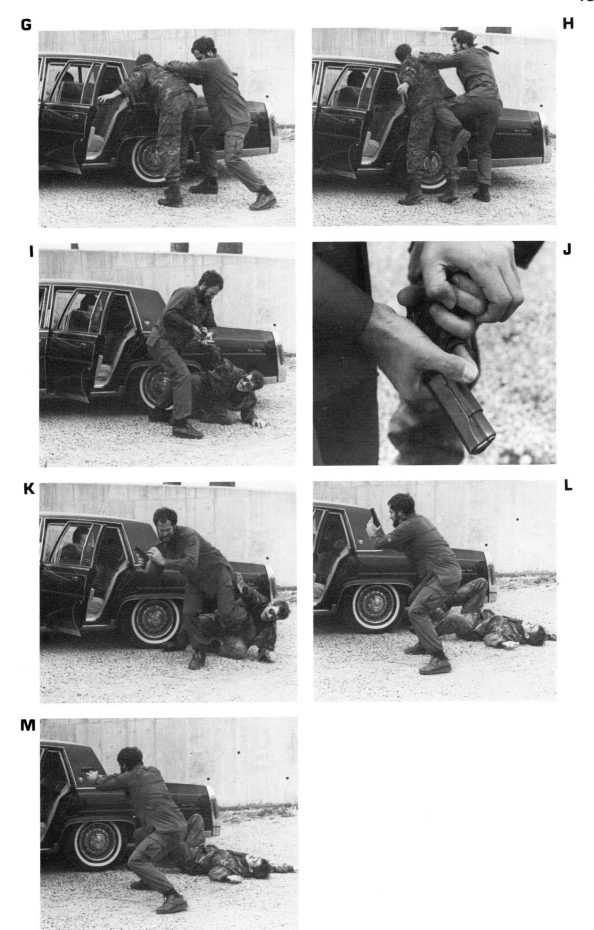

When the attacker attempts to take the defender's pistol from its holster, the defender drops his hips and begins a rearward body turn in order to jam the pistol into the holster or clear the muzzle of the gun if the attacker is too fast. Again, body movement is employed, not a mere spin-around or an attempt to grab the moving pistol. The body turn becomes the power behind a jarring elbow slam to the side of the attacker's head, while the leading arm hooks the attacker's wrist and forearm for weapon control. The defender then regains control of his weapon while subduing the attacker with a double arm bar. The defender could now easily slide his left leg back in order to force the pinned attacker to the ground.

A

Firearms cover skills, ancient and modern, follow identical principles of protection. The defender blends in with the shape and protective qualities of his cover while allowing himself the maximum amount of sighting safely possible. With the ancient *tanegashima* matchlock rifle, the defender uses the placement of the tree trunks to provide cover for his rear leg, which works to lend support for aiming the heavy weapon. In a contemporary scenario the defender uses the doorjamb structure of his automobile for cover when his driver has been stopped at a roadblock. Note that he keeps his legs inside the passenger compartment to avoid ricochet shots off the road surface and uses his knee to brace open the door. The door itself is poor cover for bullets; therefore, the defender avoids using it for protection.

B

The defender uses a *taijutsu yokonagare* sideways body drop to escape from his attacker's sight and gain protective cover. The defender drops to his seat, rolls sideways behind the tree, and emerges to where he has a clear and covered shot at his attacker. The defender's face and weapon muzzle can barely be seen to the left of the tree at its base in the final photograph of the series.

As the attacker moves in with an overhand stabbing action, the defender responds by immediately shooting out with an aggressive *hanbo* cane thrust to the attacker's throat. The defender uses a forward stepping motion along with a simultaneous extension of her cane arm in order to create the maximum possible stopping power.

The defender uses his *hanbo* cane to counter an attacker's strike by using aggressive footwork to move inside the attack and stop the clubbing swing while counterstriking the ribs. The defender then entangles the attacker's arm with a cane-assisted version of the *onikudaki* elbow and shoulder leverage technique shown in the Chapter 4 examples of the ninja's *taijutsu.* Note how the defender moves around behind the attacker to avoid his free left hand and to exert more pressure on the shoulder joint to take him down.

A

B

C

D

(Continued on next page.)

E

F

G

H

As the attacker moves forward with a lunging stab, the defender counters with an evasive step to the outside of the knife while smashing down on the blade arm with the tip of her *hanbo* cane. As a continuation of the same movement, the defender charges in with a cane-tip smash to the attacker's upper ribs. The *hanbo* is then shoved up and across the attacker's chest and used with choking leverage against the side of the attacker's neck as a means of unbalancing him. The defender uses her right knee to direct the attacker's right leg, so that she can pull him into a throw onto his back. A throat-crushing stab with the tip of the cane can then be executed if necessary.

A   **B**   **C**

D   **E**   **F**

(Continued on next page.)

6

SPIRITUAL TRAINING IN THE NINJA COMBAT METHOD

The philosophical and spiritual background of Japan's ninja was a unique blend of universal wisdom collected by the *shugenja* and *yama-bushi* warrior ascetics of the wilderness mountain ranges. Through direct experience under the guidance of a knowledgeable mentor, the fanatical warrior hermits learned the essence of the greater natural laws later embodied and codified by others in the *Shinto* ("way of the divine") perception structure. Little doctrine was expounded. Knowledge came from intimate involvement with the dangers and triumphs themselves, and conscious, aware participation was seen as the best teacher.

With the introduction of the *mikkyo* ("secret knowledge") power teachings that came from the Himalayan cultures by way of China, the wilderness seekers' base of understanding was increased twofold. The teachings brought to Japan by the holy men Saicho and Kukai in the early part of the ninth century were the perfect balancing factor to round out the mountain warriors' training concepts. The naturalist *Shinto* concept gave the ascetics a way to see the universal scheme of totality in action. The *mikkyo* teachings gave them a way to understand and thereby use the universal scheme to take them to the enlightenment they sought.

It is absolutely crucial to the student's survival to include in *ninjutsu* training what is referred to as "spiritual teachings." Indeed, training beyond the physical is 50 percent of the learning process of mastery. To approach the deadly skills that make up the authentic ninja combat method is literally to hold the power of life and death in one's hands. Unlike the conventional sport or exercise martial arts so popular today, the ninja warrior's art knows no inherent limits because it was conceived of as a means of surviving the insidious onslaught of powerful oppressors. Everything from passive wrist-grab escapes through commando-team espionage and guerilla-resistance actions is included in the curriculum of *ninjutsu* training. To learn these skills without also learning of the greater laws that govern the universe is to burden oneself with a great and dangerous imbalance.

If the skills of *ninjutsu* represent the goal of attainment for the new student, the spiritual teachings represent the code for understanding the application of the skills. It would be suicidal to become an expert in the skills of driving an automobile while ignoring the study of traffic signals and regulations. Equally lethal would be entering the depths of the ocean with

The sage Kukai, known posthumously as Kobo Daishi, who along with the sage Saicho, known as Dengyo Daishi after his death, was responsible for bringing the essence of *mikkyo* mysticism to Japan in the early 800s. *Mikkyo* power was embraced by the *shugenja* and *yamabushi* forerunners of Japan's legendary ninja.

a few diving skills while being totally ignorant of the fact that a compressed air tank will eventually run out of air or that to surface too quickly will result in painful death. To randomly throw together a collection of unknown chemicals in foolish innocence will someday produce a self-destructive explosion or fatal emission of poisonous gases. In the same way, one *must not* explore the ways of taking a life without guidance as to when such action is or is not appropriate. The lack of such guidance and wisdom in the lives of some self-styled warrior masters has led to their untimely deaths at a young age, even in modern times.

The comfort of mere religion will not suffice in this grander quest. Creeds, dogma, and doctrines actually work to interfere with the pure and unclouded perception of the universal laws in action. True spiritual power must come from direct firsthand experience. Anything less is to worship the thought of someone else's experiences. Just as adulation of the rich man or praise of the family man cannot bring one wealth or children, the adoration of past saints cannot bring saintly power to one's own life.

In one sense the term *spiritual study* is misleading in the Western world, because in the West a growing number of people believe that religion is a restrictive force based on culturally dictated concepts of "right and wrong." The fear of one's inner dictates can be a means of denying individuals much of the godly power they could tap into, had they not had the

A contemporary *mikkyo* priest performs the *goma* fire rite.

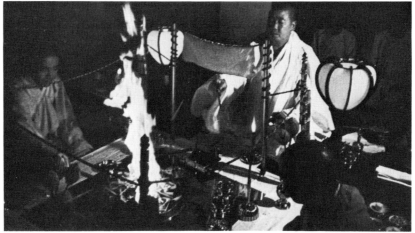

misfortune of falling into the labyrinth of myth and superstition. In the sense intended by the original *shugenja* forefathers of the ninja, spiritual study implies exploring the subtle realm that seems to be beyond the physical in order to transcend the limitations of the mechanical. Rather than approach the spiritual as an area that is above the mortal human and only to be attained from a tyrannical lord as a reward for proper behavior, the original power seekers found that knowledge of how the spiritual operates is available to anyone diligent enough to work at finding it. The original wizardry of the *shugenja* and ninja was, therefore, not magic or sorcery but pragmatic understanding and application of the universal laws in operation all around us.

Spiritual training in the *ninjutsu* combat method is not a method of religious practice, however. Indeed, students training in the *ninjutsu dojos* around the world represent all of the major religions of their own communities. Religious preference is left up to the individual. What is being sought in ninja spiritual training is the power that comes from understanding how to use those elements of life that are normally referred to as "luck," "coincidence," and "fate." It is those crucial areas beyond the mechanics of physical training that so often determine the victor and the vanquished. Therefore, the ninja seeks the total power that includes direction of these nebulous factors, which produces what the grandmaster refers to as attaining *shinshin shingan,* or "the mind and eyes of the god."

To reflect this advanced level of attainment in the ninja's art, through which the power of the will or intention is fused and made one with the physical skills of controlling the diverse aspects of the surroundings, the Japanese ancestors of today's ninja masters created an expanded concept of the *shinobi* warrior's ideal. *Ninjutsu* (the ninja's art of accomplishment) evolved into *nin-po* (the ninja's utilization of the universal laws). Far more significant than a mere semantic adjustment, the expansion from *jutsu* to *ho* (which becomes *po* when following another word) represents the elevated purpose of the warrior aspirant seeking enlightenment.

The Martial Tradition

One's reasons for studying a combat martial art should be a reflection of an understanding of the potential severity of the warrior lifestyle. Combat is certainly no game, and the practice of combat methods was not developed with idle amusement in mind. This attitude, however, seems to be growing less fashionable and becoming more and more in the minority these days.

Unfortunately, the ever-growing trend in the West, and in Japan as well, is to reduce the once-martial arts to mere contests and pastimes. A show window full of chromed trophies has become the key to drawing prospective students, champions receive ovations for moving about a gymnasium floor swinging edgeless swords in impotent imitation of warrior skills, and even tiny children now routinely strut around wearing black sash belts.

Originally, in the opening centuries of the current millenium, the martial arts of Japan were practiced for one purpose only, and that was to be capable of providing protection for one's family and loved ones in an age when there was no one else to rely on. The martial tradition was not developed for fun, any more than modern homeowners have electronic infrared security systems installed for the sake of entertainment. The purpose was pragmatic protection at heart, and the price paid for laxity in preparation and training was often the ultimate price.

Ninjutsu, or *nin-po* as it is known in its higher order, was never developed as a highly defined art with a specific range of catalogued techniques. In truth, the art's development could be seen as the product of an unfortunate necessity in a difficult age. If one wanted to know that the future of his family was as secure as it could possibly be, he was obligated to study the warrior ways and band together with neighbors who shared his foresight and concern. The initial purpose of taking on the study of the martial arts was therefore to provide for the happiness of one's family, and not at all to provide the mere excitement of involvement with violence as a means of entertainment.

In a series of five admonitions for the ninja

warriors of his *Togakure ryu,* 32nd grandmaster Shinryuken Masamitsu Toda addressed this purposefulness of warrior living on New Year's Day in the year 1891. His grandson, Toshitsugu Takamatsu, the eventual heir to the title of grandmaster of the ninja, was but two years old at the time.

The Ninja Master's Admonitions

1. Know the wisdom of being patient during times of inactivity.
2. Choose the course of justice as the path for your life.
3. Do not allow your heart to be controlled by the demands of desire, pleasure, or dependence.
4. Sorrow, pain, and resentment are natural qualities to be encountered in life. Therefore, work to cultivate the enlightenment of the immovable spirit.
5. Hold in your heart the importance of family loyalty and pursue the literary and warrior arts with balanced determination.

Shinryuken Masamitsu Toda
Togakure Ryu Ninjutsu 32nd Grandmaster
New Year's Day, 1891

Perhaps even more direct and to the point is Grandmaster Toda's grandson's observation on the meaning of this perspective in the ninja warrior's life. As a reflection of his own heart's consistency throughout a lifetime lived in a turbulent history, 33rd grandmaster Toshitsugu Takamatsu wrote his *Kofuku no Shiori.*

Essence of Happiness

The way to experience ultimate happiness is to let go of all worries and regrets and know that being happy is the most satisfying of life's feelings. Reflect back on all the progress in your life and allow the positive, creative, and joyous thoughts to outshine and overwhelm any sorrow or grief that may be lingering there in the recesses of your mind. Knowing that disease and disaster are natural parts of life is the key to overcoming adversity with a calm and happy spirit.

Happiness is waiting there in front of you. Only you can decide whether or not you choose to experience it.

Take this to heart!

Toshitsugu Takamatsu
Togakure Ryu Ninjutsu 33rd Grandmaster

According to the teachings inherited by Masaaki Hatsumi, to mature fully as a seasoned ninja warrior in all aspects of life requires 40 years of study. The first 20 years of the study are spent in learning the *omote,* or frontal aspects of the ninja's power. These are years for training in the concepts of honor, respect for superiors and parents, love and guidance

Toshitsugu Takamatsu, teacher of the current grandmaster of *ninjutsu,* Masaaki Hatsumi. Takamatsu *sensei* was nicknamed "Mongolian Tiger" by his friends and *dojo* mates in China because of his tenacity and wiry strength.

for your juniors, diligence and discipline in the training hall, and the strengths of justice, honesty, and forthrightness. The vast majority of martial arts systems stop their students' growth at this level. The ninja must progress onward through the total experience of life.

The second 20 years of your training are spent in exploring the *ura,* or rear aspects of the ninja's power. This is more often known as the "dark side" of human nature. These are years for training yourself in the ways that honor, respect, and love can be twisted out of shape and used against you and for looking at realities in which true justice and benevolence are given appearances that terrify and bewilder the masses who lack the enlightenment of perspective. Weaker souls are quick to label such wisdom as "evil" or "of demons and devils." Do not fear the strength you gain, however. Ultimately, all is godly, in that all is a part of the universe, which was created containing all. Nothing ungodly could slip in accidentally, as all is a manifestation of the god.

The 40-year experience brings you around a

full circle, having taken you through the full realm of human growth and awareness. You begin with the freshness of innocence, gather the perspectives of worldliness, and return with the wisdom of innocence. You begin empty, fill up along the way, and return empty.

Forty years of training and working at merging with the generations of the tradition who have gone before you is no guarantee that you will ever be a master of the art. The four decades merely ready you for the potential of total development. From there, how far you advance is up to your own character, personal nature, and life destiny. You will become a ninja in all the power that the word implies, if you were meant to be such.

Spiritual Methods

Concentrated awareness has always been a key tool for personal development in all of the great spiritual traditions of world history. The case is no different with the *shugendo* and *mikkyo* systems of approaching enlightenment that provided the beginnings of the ninja tradition as we know it today. Disciplined direction of consciousness through meditation training still plays a significant role in developing the warrior skills of the *ninjutsu* combat method.

Meditation training is working with directing the consciousness toward a particular focus and then holding it there as long as is needed or desired. The point of focus could be a particular thought to be held, question to be pondered, energy to be directed, or sight to be monitored. Ultimately, through repetitive training and practice, the meditative state develops to the point at which total immersion takes place. The observer, action of observing, and object of observation all lose their independent aspects and blend as one single flowing process.

This total immersion is not necessarily as mysterious or otherworldly as it might sound in a written description. Football fans will recognize this blending of subject and object in the intense feelings of being totally wrapped up in the last remaining minutes of a tie game being watched on television. In effect, the watcher is no longer independent from the watching, and the electronic device before him ceases to exist. The viewer becomes a part of the second-to-second flow emotionally, intellectually, and even physically as he moves in rhythm with the images on the screen, totally in tune and a part of the pain and triumph that is in reality a remote television broadcast. Others will recognize the immersion in an experience in a movie theater, while reading a gripping novel, or while observing a joy or catastrophe in real life. We literally become the experience.

This immersion experience is foreign to few people. Most of us can recall having been totally absorbed by something at least once in our lives. The difficulty, however, lies in training our minds and bodies to allow us to create that total immersion at will and on command. For that kind of power, meditation practice is necessary.

The consciousness can be directed inward or outward, depending on where the awareness needs to be. Meditation can be a means of tuning out all physical distractions and superfluous thoughts in order to center oneself and permit the inner voice of intuition and inspiration to be heard. This method of inner directed concentration is typical of Zen-style meditation. Conversely, meditation can also be a means of tuning out all inner impressions and rambling thoughts in order to extend oneself and become a part of the surrounding actions or environmental states. This method of outward directed concentration is typical of tantric-style meditation. Both are equal parts of balanced training in the powers of concentration and spiritual development.

This inner and outer awareness direction is symbolized by the two great mandala designs of the ninja's *mikkyo*. The *kongokai* mandala is the so-called right-hand view of the structure of the universe and represents the natural laws as they are reflected in the spiritual or "ultimate truth" realm. It is the "god's eye view," or what the universe would look like from the outside if such sight were possible. The *taizokai* mandala is the so-called left-hand view of the structure of the universe and represents the natural laws as they are manifested in the physical or

The *kongokai,* or "diamond spiritual realm," mandala, which provides a schematic diagram of the universe from the outside in.

The *taizokai,* or "material womb realm," mandala, which provides a schematic diagram of the universe as we know it from the inside out.

"material reality" realm. It is the "being's eye view," or what the universe looks like from the inside.

In actuality both mandala designs reflect the same thing, only from two distinctly different perspectives. There is, of course, only one universe in the sense of its being the total collection of all that is. Only our varying perspectives create the two dramatically differing impressions, just as we can see only the heads or tails side of the identical coin at any given moment.

As a simple analogy to illustrate these two perspectives, you could hold in your hand two photographs of a house, one taken from the frontyard, looking through a window into the living room, and another taken from inside the kitchen, looking through the living room and out the window to the frontyard. The two scenes would appear to be totally different, and yet they would in truth merely be two reflections of the identical residence. It is the same with the "inner" and "outer" cosmic views provided by the two mandalas.

Of course, aspirants to enlightenment use the two mandalas as aids to meditation on a higher level in their practice of *mikkyo* as a

spiritual method. However, in this volume the two mandala concepts will be restricted to their applications as symbols for training in combat self-protection skills alone.

The Practice

The initial procedures for both inner-directed and outer-directed meditation are identical in that they work to center the concentration on a desired point of focus. The following steps should be followed as a means of approaching both types of meditation skills.

1. Choose an appropriate location for your training, where you are not likely to be bothered or disturbed by external factors or other persons. Ideally, you would like to find a place that is sensually neutral. It should be comfortable but not sleep-inducing, neither too hot nor too cool, neither too bright nor too dark, neither too noisy nor too quiet. Any place that is relatively free of distractions without being an unnerving sensual vacuum will serve as an effective meditation training area.

2. Settle yourself in a comfortable seated position, not too close to anyone else if you are doing group meditation training. Maintain at least slightly more than an arm's length distance from others. Draw your legs in, fold them to support your body trunk. If needed or desired, a small firm pillow or folded blanket can be used to lift your seat slightly so that you will feel no temptation to strain forward for balance.

There is no one absolutely best seat for meditation training. Different bodies will be comfortable with different arrangements. Some of the more popular seated postures are illustrated in the accompanying photos.

3. Straighten your spine and then lean for-

Relaxed Folded-Leg Seat. Pull the legs in toward your body comfortably with both ankles on the ground. There is no need to cross the legs.

Japanese *Seiza* Kneeling. Pull your feet together beneath your seat and rest your hips on your heels. The toes should be pointing straight back.

Half-Lotus Seat. Fold your legs with one leg and foot resting on top of the other.

Full Lotus Seat. Fold your legs in an intertwined position where both feet rest on top of the thighs. This allows the knees to rest flat on the floor.

***Fudoza* Heel Seat. Fold the left foot beneath your hips and sit on the flattened ankle while pulling your right leg in for balance and support.**

ward and back, side to side, and twist around in your seated position a few times to get yourself situated. You will be sitting still for several minutes, so take a moment to work out any stiffness or discomfort before it manifests itself.

4. Lay or fold your hands in your lap, lower your chin slightly to straighten and align the vertebrae in your neck, and lower your eyelids to a relaxed closed state.

5. Breathe in deeply, as deeply as you can, and totally fill your lungs. Hold your breath, and with your lungs filled to capacity, relax the bones and muscles downward around the air held in your chest. Retain your frame in this relaxed position and allow the air to leave your lungs. Only your stomach should move if you have filled your lungs and totally relaxed your body frame around them. Repeat the process again once or twice to be sure that the motion of your breathing will not disturb you later on during the meditation.

6. Allow the breath to move in and out of your body through your nose. Breathe naturally and fully; do not attempt to force or control the breathing at all.

7. In a relaxed and emotionlessly detached manner, watch the breathing process. Feel, hear, taste; in all ways and with all senses, be aware of the breathing in and breathing out pattern. With each exhalation, imagine yourself dropping further and further into a relaxed state of centeredness.

8. As an exercise for developing your ability to focus on a single mental process, you can practice counting your breath cycles, or visualizing symbolic images that fit the rhythm of your breathing. Both exercises are deceptively simple in that they are designed to provide a simple objective that can be monitored for consistency. It is not at all difficult to tell whether your mind is staying with the exercise or wandering off aimlessly.

For breath counting, begin at zero and increase the mental number in your mind by one each time you breathe out. Continue from one through nine and then begin over again at one. Hold fast to the numeric progression with all your attention and relax into the task of counting.

For image visualization, mentally create a vivid impression of an ocean shore as the surf breaks in and pulls out. Each outgoing breath should mirror the crash of the waves on the shore, and each incoming breath should mirror the retreat and buildup of a new wave. Hold fast to the rhythmic cycle with all your attention and allow the soothing image to take you to relaxation.

9. When first beginning your meditation training, work for a period of 10 minutes each day. Gradually extend the length of your sessions until they reach 20 minutes in length and you are experiencing noticeable results in terms of mind and body relaxation and command of your own awareness and concentration.

Once concentration direction abilities have been developed, or at least enhanced, you can move on to the application of meditation skills toward *ninjutsu* combat training. Using the two mandala concepts, we can reduce the scale from cosmic to human and apply the same perspectives for gaining the necessary insights. We can use the meditative awareness for an inward-directed view to listen to or dictate to the subconscious. We can also use the same meditation principles for an outward-directed view, in order to pick up information from or tune into harmony with our surrounding environment.

Visualization

Once you have gained mastery over the nine fundamental steps, inward-directed meditation can be used for a variety of internal enhancement methods, including relaxation, energy channeling, and awareness centering. In this example one method for the practice of visualization is described to show the means by which the subconscious is tapped.

In the meditation state, use your imagination

to create a mental image of yourself and a training partner in front of you. See the image vividly, with all details intact. Sense the tension and potential explosive action as though the image were a real physical confrontation. See, smell, taste, hear all the aspects of the scene in order to make the image as real as possible.

In your mind, see your training partner fly forward at you with a right fist punch to the face. See yourself respond by shifting back and to the right, inside of his punch and out of his range. As his fist reaches out after you, see your own arm rolling up and out, sending your clenched fist into the wrist of your training partner's attacking arm. Upon impact, see his arm fly back away from you in pain and shock. Your defensive backpedaling footwork turns into an attacking charge, and you see yourself sailing forward with a powerful right-hand counterstrike that knocks your attacker backward.

As you replay the scene over and over again in your mind, strive to capture the total essence of realism. Experience the emotions as though the exchange were a physical reality. Allow your breathing to fit the mental motions. Feel the tensing and relaxing of your muscles. Above all else, hold on to the awareness of the success of your counter. Allow your mind to consciously (and subconsciously) absorb the fact that you handled the attack perfectly. Your timing and distancing were perfect. Your power application was perfect. The rhythm of the exchange and your conversion from defense to attack were perfect. Remember that you had the experience and you handled it perfectly. The skill is yours. Remember that you have experienced the reality of knowing that the skill is yours.

Supplement your physical training with the mental visualization process to get a better grip on each new technique to be mastered. As much as possible, accompany all training sessions with at least a few moments of visualized reinforcement to shorten the time necessary to bring physical skills and mental realizations into harmony as one process. In effect, confidently believing that you can use the technique and perfecting the technique to the point at which you have confidence in it are mirror reflections of the same process.

External Awareness

Once you have gained mastery over the nine fundamental steps, outward-directed meditation can be used for a variety of external awareness methods, including consciousness of surroundings, attention to detail, attunement of thoughts with others, perception of danger, and decision making. In this example one method for practice of consciousness extension is described to show the means by which the awareness can be directed to where it is needed. The exercise should be performed with a training partner, preferably outside in a natural setting.

In the meditative state, with your eyes closed, use your imagination to create eight "cone-shaped" zones of awareness radiating out from your position as the hub. There will be a zone in front of you, to your right front, to your right side, to your right rear, behind you, to your left rear, to your left side, and to your left front.

Moving slowly from zone to zone, monitor each sector for all natural impressions that come to you. Make a note of all sounds, breezes, smells, vibrations, feelings, and sensations. You are working at becoming comfortable with all that is there. Later, anything that disturbs what you have come to know will trigger an unconscious signal that something has changed and perhaps requires your attention.

After several minutes of relaxing into harmony with your surroundings, your training partner will approach you slowly and as silently as possible from whichever direction he chooses. His object is to move to a spot where he can reach out and touch you without being detected beforehand. You will use all your senses (except sight) and impressions to locate and point out your training partner as quickly as you can. When you feel that you have detected his approach, point in that direction and open your eyes to verify your perception.

Do not rush through the exercise. Take the time necessary to accustom yourself to your surroundings. At its highest level the exercise works because you have become a part of the environment and can perceive anything that affects that environment. If you rush at the exercise, you will be limited to the energy draining process of straining at listening for every strange or suspicious sound. A skilled and patient stalker will get you every time under those conditions.

Why Spiritual Work?

You would not be satisfied with a bank in which your money was safe "most of the time." You would not settle for home drinking water that was "usually" pure. You would not be confident with a land deed or title that was "pretty much" recognized as genuine. In the same light, a person who is relying on martial skills as a life-directing and possibly lifesaving aspect of overall capability will refuse to settle for a system that can quickly be mastered by anyone and that relies on mere speed and power for supremacy.

The thorough combatant will rely on every possible advantage to bring victory and security. There will always be someone else out there who is younger, faster, stronger, and in possession of more tricks. Therefore, the ninja warrior takes his or her training beyond the bounds of conventional limitations into realms that few others think to include in their martial regimens. For this reason, the art of the ninja combat method has survived and thrived for more than a millenium in Japan and is now blossoming into an international source of personal guidance and power.

INDEX